CHINA AS No 1

By the Same Author

On China
Business Guide to China (co-authored with Li Dao Ran, 1996)
Banking and Finance in China (co-authored with
Stephen X. M. Lu, 1996)
Negotiating in China—36 Strategies (1995)
China Inc. (1995)
The China Forex Guide (co-authored with Pang Ji Ying, 1994)
Intellectual Property & Technology Transfer in China (1994)
*Foreign Exchange Controls in China: A Strategic Guide for Corporate
Survival* (1993)
Foreign Exchange Controls and Strategies for the PRC (1989)
Intellectual Property Law in the PRC (1988)

On Indo-China
Vietnam: Banking and Finance (1995)
Intellectual Property & Technology Transfer in Vietnam (1994)
The Vietnam Customs Guide (1994)
Banking and Finance in Indochina (1992)
Foreign Investment and Trade Law in Vietnam (1992)
Investment in the Lao PDR (co-authored with
Neill T. Macpherson, 1991)

CHINA AS No 1
THE NEW SUPERPOWER
TAKES CENTRE STAGE

LAURENCE J. BRAHM

Butterworth-Heinemann Asia,
an imprint of Reed Academic Publishing Asia,
a division of Reed Elsevier (Singapore) Pte Ltd.
1 Temasek Avenue
#17–01 Millenia Tower
Singapore 039192

ISBN 9810067976

Cover design by Luna Park Advertising Team
Typeset by Post Typesetters
Printed by International Press Co. Pte Ltd.

PREFACE

I remember when I first arrived in China. It was summer, 1981. The airport was baking in a flat heat. The road from Capital Airport into Beijing seemed long. The bus broke down several times. My first stop, like most foreigners in those days, was at the Friendship Store. I bought a Coke. It was imported and cost one dollar. That would have been more than any Chinese at that time could have ever conceived of spending on a drink. Anyway, in those days, no ordinary Chinese citizens were permitted to enter the Friendship Store.

I lived in Tianjin, one of the last bastions of leftism. Nankai University, where I studied, looked as if it had been through a war. Ceilings had fallen in and rubble was everywhere. Students walked beside the lake near the library in the evenings reading Marx. When I asked what had happened to all the buildings, they just whispered, 'Terrible things have happened'. No-one said any more.

I bought a bicycle. As the hot summer dragged on, it fell apart. It seemed that each day a piece had to be replaced. Eventually, the bike I finished up with was different from the one I bought.

I met rebellious artists. They took me to their homes and showed me wild modern explosions painted on the back of Mao posters. Then they rolled everything up carefully, put them back under the bed, and showed me politely to the door.

Most people lived in shacks made of rubble. The Tangshan earthquake which shook China in 1976, the year of Mao's death, had destroyed many homes. People used the debris for makeshift shelters which were everywhere. Then Chairman Hua Guofeng visited and told the people to clean up the mess and rebuild the city. But he did not say how they were to do it.

There was something new on everyone's lips—it was the words 'free market'. Some bold peasants brought vegetables and sometimes little cloth handkerchiefs of peanuts, squatted on the kerbside and sold them. They could keep the money themselves. It was the beginning of the free market. Across from the free market, people lined up each afternoon at the State-run stores. They had tickets to exchange for staples. Every day, everywhere, the things were the same—that is, if anything was available. Everyone was happy if something was available. I remember being with a classmate when we found a small roasted baby chicken in the window of one of these stores. We bought and ate it; we were very happy to have something that simple.

It seemed that every single item was used and reused. When a pen ran dry, the students found a way to put water in it and make more ink come out; every scrap of paper was written on until there was no white left. Nothing in this society was wasted.

There was a forlorn innocence. Sometimes in the street at night I did simple magic tricks which I had brought from home. People would laugh and ask me to perform again, and again, and again. They never seemed to get tired of the same tricks.

If I paid one *mao* more than the stated price for something, the vendor would chase me all over the city to give me the change.

Then it came time to leave Nankai University. I was not aware that, over the next 15 years, I would watch China grow and change. It did not seem possible that these things would change. The thought did not even occur to me as I sold my bike—on the black market.

Sixteen years later, Tianjin is unrecognisable to me. I have lost all sense of direction: the shacks are all gone; the rubble is that of massive construction sites and I am in the shadows of skyscrapers. The wild artists are all working for slick advertising companies. Foreign students no longer have to forage for baby chickens. They will find McDonalds on most street corners in the major cities of China. The Hard Rock Cafe in Beijing booms with accelerated culture shock every night of the week until 2.00 a.m. Ordinary citizens can go to all the new department stores, boutiques, and even the Friendship Store, which rings of nostalgia. Everything is available and people seem to be able to afford anything.

No-one will give you change if they think they can get away with it. There is a commercial tenacity in China today which makes Hong Kong look like *laissez-faire* Sunday School. The single dominating ideology is money . . . and Mao. His picture dangles from the mirror of virtually every small taxi. 'In the countryside, the peasants say he can change the weather and stop the floods,' explains one taxi driver. 'We keep his picture because we know he can prevent traffic accidents.'

Traffic chokes the cities. City planners are planning new roads to be built over old narrow alleys. The culture and old lifestyles of these alleys are bulldozed into oblivion, the cost of development. The developers run off to 'Rich and Powerful People Hot Pot City Restaurant' for dinner; after dinner they go to karaoke, and then massage, and then to the disco.

In front of television cameras in a five-star hotel in Beijing, representatives of an American trade mission are saying, 'China has to change its system more quickly . . . they have to accept free trade . . . they have to play fair . . . they're getting better but it's not enough. We will have to slam sanctions on them if they don't change their economy and accept free trade.' Where the hotel stands there was countryside 15 years ago and peasants squatted in the dark eating *guotou*, a harsh cornmeal crust which was their main staple then. Tonight, as the American trade representatives drone on, the flashing lights of Changan Avenue outside look more like Tokyo's Ginza.

All development has its costs. With each cost there is some development. The leadership of China, on the eve of Liberation in 1949, was a leadership of battleworn visionaries. The leadership of China, on the eve of the twenty-first century, is a leadership of pragmatists who have struggled for survival, with a clear vision of the future. The West has not fought China's battles, has not experienced a struggle of survival or survived a Cultural Revolution, yet continues to criticise China. Many modern Western leaders do not have a clear vision of the future of their own country; how can they have a vision of China's? Perhaps they fear China, its size and its potential dominance. However, they reinforce their fears through misinterpretations of events in China without taking the time to understand the forces driving this new dynamic energy of China.

I feel distraught when I meet people who are determined to believe that everything in China is negative, and that the Government is heading towards a Soviet Union-style disintegration. They seem reluctant to face the fact that some very positive and creative developments are occurring in China, that China is becoming capitalist and socialist at the same time, and that somehow this blend might work.

The Chinese seem to believe that, if it works, then it is *keyi* (OK). People in other countries seem to think that the Chinese should believe in something else; they (and unfortunately their policymakers and diplomats) seem to only believe what their own newspapers write about China, and nothing more. I remember, as a student in China 15 years ago, reading the newspapers. They criticised Taiwan, saying basically the same things Western newspapers said about the Soviet Union. I asked myself then, 'If American newspapers are supposed to tell the truth, and Chinese newspapers are supposed to be full of propaganda, but both say the same things, then maybe the Chinese newspapers have some truth and the American papers a lot of propaganda?'

It is the intention that this book should open the eyes of the West to the dynamics and magnitude of what is occurring in China today, and the positive effects that these events will have on the world in the next century. Maybe on another level, there is a faint hope that this book, by presenting the facts from China's perspective, will lead to some introspection, a quiet self-questioning of entrenched beliefs, and thereby prompt calls for badly needed economic and political reforms in other countries.

The chapters of this book are divided into three parts followed by a conclusion. Although each chapter is complete in itself, the reader will benefit from reading all the chapters in each part.

Part I Policies is intended to set out the parameters which have become the basis of China's current economic and political reforms, and their underlying principles and values.

Part II Reforms selects a number of critical macro-reforms and looks at how far China has come over the past 15 years to arrive at where it is today.

Part III Greater China looks at the inherent pragmatism of Chinese in seeing reunification as a keystone in closing chapters of the past and advancing Chinese commercial interests into the future.

Critics may comment that the views in this book are pro-China. This is only partially correct. The views in this book present a positive and hopeful look at many of the hard and difficult reforms which China has undertaken, presenting with optimism the hopes and vision which a lot of people in China hold for the direction in which the economy is now running. This is not to say that China will not have many difficulties with which to contend: many seemingly unsolvable domestic problems will have to be solved, maybe with varying results which may be hard for some to accept or comprehend. Mistakes will inevitably be made and difficulties will persist. Nevertheless, China will have come into its own.

CONTENTS

PART III

GREATER CHINA

Photographs (between pages 128 and 129)

1. Yanan, 1942. Mao Zedong lecturing cadres in front of his cave shelter. Yanan became Mao's proletarian 'Garden of Eden' where he lectured a new philosophy of political compassion and egalitarianism, the 'spirit of Yanan'.

2. Yanan, 1944. From left to right, Marshal Zhu De, Mao and General Wang Zhen reviewing Red Army guerilla forces as they come closer to victory over the Kuomintang. While Chiang Kai-shek took refuge in Shanghai and Nanjing, Mao and his comrades endured the harsh conditions of Yanan, gaining the support of the peasant masses.

3. Yanan, 1944. Mao greeting Hurley Stilwell, appointed by President Roosevelt to lead the Dixie Mission to China. Marshal Zhu De (at left) looks on. Mao wished to forge a close alliance with the United States, not the Soviet Union. His approaches to the West were, however, spurned by the anti-communist bloc in Washington.

4. Shanghai, 1951. Mao dining with Rong Yiren (at left). While other tycoons fled to Hong Kong or Taiwan, Rong, the 'Red Capitalist', supported Mao when the communists came to power. Deng Xiaoping rewarded Rong's allegiance with the mandate to establish China International Trust and Investment Corporation (CITIC) as the corporate arm of the State Council. Rong is now China's Vice Chairman of State.

5. Beijing, 1966. Mao acknowledging Red Guards atop Tiananmen. The young people of the 1960s sought to revive the idealised 'spirit of Yanan' by embracing a 'non-materialist' culture.

6. Beijing, 1996. Young citizens of Beijing today are absorbed in a 'materialist' culture, exemplified by these scenes in a Beijing disco.

7. Beijing, 1975. Premier Zhou Enlai addressing the National People's Congress in the Great Hall of the People. Making what was to be his last major speech before he succumbed to cancer, Premier Zhou announced the 'Four Modernisations', a new policy focusing on agriculture, industry, science and technology, and national defence.

8. Beijing, 1978. Chen Yun and Deng Xiaoping (right) at the Eleventh Party Congress, at which Deng consolidated his power and took control of China's economy. This meeting also marked the commencement of the open door policy. Although Deng's pragmatic approach differed from that of Chen, both men worked together on developing and implementing economic reform.

9. 1984. Vice Premier Wan Li (left) chatting with a rural family. Wan Li implemented agricultural reform experiments in Anhui Province concurrently with Zhao Ziyang's reforms in Sichuan. He went on to serve as Vice Premier while Zhao became Premier. Although retired, Wan Li is still an influence in China and is a member of Deng's innermost circle.

10. Beijing, 1987. Deng speaking at the Thirteenth Party Congress when he broke with traditional ideology by announcing that China must support socialism, but '. . . not leap into socialism if we are not there yet'. Zhao Ziyang also commented: 'China has not yet reached the stage of communism . . . only an initial stage of socialism'. This meeting was significant for the views expressed on both ideology and the direction that China should take in the implementation of economic reforms.

11. Beijing, 1989. Jiang Zemin and Deng Xiaoping at the Thirteenth Plenary Session of the Chinese Communist Party, at which Jiang emerged as General Secretary of the Party. While Jiang has since been building his own power base, Deng remains a strong influence in the decision-making process.

12. Shenzhen, 1992. Deng Xiaoping during his famous 'Southern Inspection Trip' which was, in fact, a well-calculated move to revive China's economy by initiating and encouraging further liberal reform. Deng hailed the success of Shenzhen, China's booming Special Economic Zone across from Hong Kong, and reaffirmed his theory of China's 'socialist market economy with Chinese characteristics'. General Yang Shangkun (at Deng's left shoulder) was in charge of security during the trip.

13. Beijing, 1993. First Vice Premier Zhu Rongji, dubbed by Western observers as China's 'economic czar', has overseen the implementation of a complex series of banking and monetary reforms which has modernised China's financial system while at the same time bringing the Renminbi to the threshold of convertibility. In 1993, he took over as Governor of the People's Bank of China (the central bank) and steered the economy through a critical inflationary period. Within three years, he has succeeded in bringing the level of inflation down to below that of growth.

14. Beijing, 1994. China's Minister of Foreign Trade and Economic Cooperation, Wu Yi, and the late US Secretary of Commerce, Ronald Brown, signing a Sino–US trade cooperation agreement.

15. 1995. Jiang Zemin, as Chairman of the Central Military Commission, on an inspection tour with the Vice Chairmen of the Commission. From left, Chairman Jiang Zemin, General Liu Huaqing, General Zhang Zhen, official, General Zhang Wannian and General Chi Haotian. While Liu Huaqing and Zhang Zhen are strong supporters of Deng, observers say that Jiang Zemin appointed Chi Haotian and Zhang Wannian as Vice Chairmen to strengthen his own power base.

16. Beijing, 1995. Members of the powerful State Council at a press conference. Premier Li Peng (at lectern) taking questions from Chinese and foreign journalists during the National Party Congress. Looking on are, from left, Vice Premiers Wu Bangguo, Qian Jichen, Zhu Rongji, Zou Jiahua, Li Lanqing and Jiang Chunyun.

17. Beijing, 1996. First Vice Premier Zhu Rongji chatting with Jiang Zemin (centre). At right is Central Military Commission Vice Chairman, Liu Huaqing, and next to him is Li Ruihuan, Chairman of the Chinese People's Political Consultative Conference. On Zhu Rongji's right is Hu Jintao, the youngest member of the Communist Party Central Committee Standing Committee, seen as a rising star on China's political scene.

18. Beijing, 1996. The Standing Committee of the Central Committee of the Chinese Communist Party entering the Great Hall of the People during the National Party Congress in March. At front from left: Qiao Shi (Chairman of the National People's Congress), Jiang Zemin (General Secretary of the Party, Chairman of State and Chairman of the Central Military Commission), Li Peng (Premier of the State Council) and Li Ruihuan (Chairman of the Chinese People's Political Consultative Conference). Behind, from left: Rong Yiren (Vice Chairman of State), Liu Huaqing (First Vice Chairman of the Central Military Commission), Zhu Rongji (First Vice Premier of the State Council) and Hu Jintao (President of the Central Committee Party School). (Rong Yiren is the only person shown here who is not a member of the Standing Committee.)

ACKNOWLEDGMENTS

The brown wrinkle of fallen leaves can be heard in the midnight breeze on the doorstep. This is the sound of Beijing in mid-autumn. For much of the past five years I have lived in this Qing period courtyard house, which was the former home of Hua Guofeng (Mao's chosen successor). In the winter months, the Mongolian winds cut dry and sandy through the narrow *hutong* alleys outside, which form a labyrinth in the centre of Beijing. This gives the courtyard a sense of solitude. That is why I chose to live here throughout the writing of this book.

It is said that the decision to arrest the Gang of Four was taken in this courtyard during a midnight meeting between Hua Guofeng, Wang Dongxing and Marshal Ye Jianying in 1976. This event, exactly 20 years ago, was the catalyst for a series of momentous changes which have brought China to where it is today.

Understanding China is a misleading notion. As much as I have tried to spend the past 15 years of my life understanding China, I am always amazed at how much I do not know. There are very few people—including many Chinese—who can say honestly that they really understand the different forces and the momentum behind these forces driving China and the Chinese people today.

Aware of my limitations as an outsider observing wave after wave of developments in this vast and complicated society, I have tried to piece together aspects of life and events in China to form a picture which I hope will give readers a somewhat different perspective from those most often portrayed in the media. At least this has been my objective.

I have closely followed China's developments and reforms over the past 15 years. This book represents a collection of my thoughts over this period. It is therefore appropriate that I thank a number of individuals who have influenced these thoughts and who have encouraged and helped me in the writing of this book.

I must first thank Howard Coats, my long-time mentor and friend in Hong Kong who helped me to crystallise this idea in 1993. I also owe a great thanks to Thomas Hon Wing Polin of *Asiaweek* magazine who reviewed this book and provided me with his own insights, knowledge and advice. I also owe exceptional thanks to my editor Liz Goodman who had the patience to work through the text of this book. I would also like to thank Craig Smith of the *Asian Wall Street Journal* for his comments which helped me improve the text, Sydney Shapiro for his inspiration and endorsement as one of the original 'old China hands', and Louise De Rosario, who encouraged me to pursue and complete this project at a time when the road ahead seemed quite long.

I would also like to thank Victor Hao Li of the East–West Centre in Hawaii and C.Y. Chang of the Chinese University of Hong Kong who both helped me formulate my early framework for 'reading' China; and both Wing K. Yung, with whom I have had an ongoing 15-year philosophical dialogue on China developments, and Zoher Abdoolcarim of *Asiaweek*, who has encouraged my writing on the subject over this period.

Additional thanks are owed to Michael Yu Xiaoyu, Robert Wang Yong, Chang Hu and Li Mingde who have contributed to my understanding of current conditions and patterns of thinking in China. Special thanks to my old classmate, Qu Jianxiong, one of China's up-and-coming modern artists, for his own philosophical perspectives on life in China today.

I owe tremendous thanks to the Naga Group staff who have helped me with the preparation of this text, particularly Vera Wan of Naga's Hong Kong office who handled all administrative matters related to this book, Cat Law who developed the graphs and tables, and Julia Zhang who helped me with my chronic computer problems in Beijing.

In the research for this book, I owe special thanks to Bobby Zhang of Naga's Beijing office for his knowledge of economic and structural reforms in China today, Stephen X. M. Lu of Naga's Shanghai office for his insights, as well as Wang Bangmin and Wendy Zhao

Wenli for their patient and dedicated research. Special thanks must also go to New China News Agency for kindly supplying the photographs that appear in this book.

There are also many friends of mine who are serving in official capacities in the various offices of China's Government today. Without the ongoing guidance and insights of these friends, this book would not have been possible at all. As I cannot name so many individuals in this particular context, I can only express great gratitude for their help, patient time and encouragement. In fact, I am indebted to these friends.

As much of the material for this book has been drawn from personal observation and contacts, or from Chinese Government documents and media reports published in Chinese, it is not possible for me to provide citations in the text. For those who wish to read more on the subject of China, I am pleased to suggest a number of general English-language references that I have found useful: *China: The Next Economic Superpower*, by William H. Overholt (1993); *Mao* (1993) and *Madame Mao* (1992) both by Ross Terrill; *The New Emperors*, by Harrison Salisbury (1991); *Dragon Lady* by Sterling Seagrave (1992); and *Eldest Son*, by Han Suyin (1994). These books I recommend as useful historical references for understanding modern China. I also recommend reading *Dateline—China Rising*, published by the Overseas Press Club of America (1996 Special Issue), which contains a selection of journalistic essays providing an excellent perspective on China today.

I would also like to thank the publisher, David Catterall of Reed Academic, for having the faith to support and undertake this project.

Laurence J. Brahm
Beijing
October 1996

古爲今用，
洋爲中用。

Let the past serve the present,
let foreign things serve China.

—Mao Zedong

INTRODUCTION

Western perceptions of China are bound by a series of misconceptions and prejudices which, when combined, form the basic framework through which the events and changes occurring within China are misinterpreted. Unfortunately, this framework is not easy to dismantle, as it stems from centuries of misleading information.

PERCEPTIONS

Perceptions of China began to be formed 800 years ago when the Mongolian hordes tore across the Siberian plains, through what is today Russia and Eastern Europe. This, historically, was the 'West's' first real encounter with the 'East'. The Mongolian invasion left in its wake wasted cities and populations—the hit-and-run strategy of conquest adopted by what was basically a nomadic people. The Mongolian conquest stunned Europe; the Mongolians seemed ruthless, unstoppable and undefeatable.

In the early thirteenth century, Europe was essentially inward-looking, wrapped in self-conviction of its own superiority. Christian dogma had already become the basis of the European world view for analysing all existence and justifying all political means, to whatever end. It was the only framework at that time through which the West could interpret the events occurring in the East. This contrasted with the Mongolian perception of the world—Mongolian expansion meant the absorption of cultures. With each conquest, a new bounty of artisans and scholars was sent to the Mongolian capital at Quaratum and assimilated into the growing empire. The result was a mind-set of religious tolerance: there came to be Christian and Muslim, as well as Buddhist, Mongolian Khanates. This tolerance of ideals stands in stark contrast with the pettiness of the various European Christian sects which fought so bitterly amongst each other to defend mere theoretical differences or interpretations of theology.

The Mongolians, a race of nomadic warriors, disdained agricultural peoples. They viewed Western culture as being what it was at that time—a peasant society enduring the yoke of feudalism reinforced by the yoke of religion. From the Mongolian perspective, it was only worthy of being trashed and ruled. The West saw the Mongol threat purely in theological terms: the Mongolians were people of darkness bent on destroying Christendom. Despite all factual evidence to the contrary, European maps of Asia at that time depicted a land of dog-headed men and other assorted monsters, perpetuating the myth of fear and further shrouding all things Eastern in hedonism and mystery.

The simple fact of the matter was that the Mongolians were superior militarily to the Europeans through strategic application and technique, not superior mass or strength. Even at this formative stage of European culture, military might was seen in terms of numbers only.

Battles were determined according to the amount of mass put on the battlefield, not the skill of the warriors. Armour became the key to war: the more armoured men on horseback who clashed with the enemy, the more armoured men would be likely to be still standing on the field when the battle was over. Armour was purchased with money, and the system of knighthood became a system of feudal economics: give the population religion to keep them focused on labour, tax their labour and use the tax to purchase or manufacture armaments to prevent uprisings and expand territory. These principles continued into modern times in Europe, and in turn become the basis of the military–corporate–government symbiosis which would develop in the twentieth century, to be dubbed the 'new industrial State' by liberal economist, John Kenneth Galbraith.

The Mongolians by contrast were adaptable, and not bound by the constraints and inflexibility created by armour on the battlefield. Whereas the Europeans lined up in serried ranks like Campbell's soup cans, unable to turn to counter the changing movements of the enemy, the Mongolians were swift, setting ambushes and traps, and forever outflanking and running rings around an enemy as physically constrained by its armour as it was by its philosophy and framework for understanding the non-Western world.

When the Mongolian threat subsided, Europe breathed, and feudalism continued. The dark ages, however, began to brighten when, in times of peace, Marco Polo visited Kublai Khan, and brought back with him the refinements of culture which had already become an accepted basis of life in China, but which remained unheard of in Europe. With culture he brought new technology—gunpowder. It was the European exploitation of the potential of this single item—gunpowder—which catapulted Europe out of its own self-imprisoning armour.

Four centuries later, the Europeans, having perfected the application of gunpowder, would venture to the gates of China. Their military technology would for the first time in history be superior to what the East had to offer. For the Europeans, this meant a new basis for confrontation—the scales would be tipped in favour of the West. The memory and mystery of the Mongolian hordes, however, would remain unchanged.

By this time, the Manchurians, not the Mongolians, ruled China. Like their predecessors, however, they absorbed Chinese culture, or rather, they were absorbed into it. The China which the West 'discovered' was a world of refinement and culture consistent with the marvels which inspired Marco Polo. Coveted by the West, these refinements became a target for possession.

As their mind-set remained unchanged, the Europeans justified their actions through religious dogma and feelings of superiority. The missionaries saw a vast population of 'heathens' to convert; the politicians encouraged and gave full support to this view as it suited perfectly their objectives of economic colonisation of the East. With the growth of Western industrialisation, the West was looking for new markets into which it could expand and eventually control. Whether its philosophy was based on religious dogma and the alleged mission of religious conversion, or on a new political dogma and a mission of political conversion, or both, the West consistently rationalised its actions in China throughout the 1800s and into the 1900s. Although the veneer might change, the mind-set stays the same. The perpetuation of old myths from a Mongolian China served to provide a basis for Western governments to justify their attempts to manipulate and control China politically with the objective of extracting from China as much as possible economically.

In the 1960s, nascent American policies of political 'containment' were premised on fears that Chinese communists would spread throughout South-East Asia. In his domino theory, John Foster Dulles saw the 'red threat' working its way from Indo-China south, to eventually encompass Australia and New Zealand. American policy toward Communist China in the 1960s was heavily flavoured with Hollywood-style hype resulting in a deepening of Western paranoia over a perceived thirteenth century-style Mongolian expansion projected into the twentieth century. The domino theory of a mere 30 years ago may seem absurd today. Nevertheless, in its trade relations with China, Washington still seems to have an image of China surging over its borders.

It is China's objective to develop its economy and raise the standard of living of its own people—something which should be in line with Western values. An import substitution/export promotion model has been adopted for this purpose along the already successful models of Singapore and, to some extent, Taiwan. However, there is still the perception that China's growing mega-economy is a threat of Mongolian proportions.

When covering China, the focus of the Western media is on the odd situation, the extreme occurrence, and mainstream thought or activity is not reported on. There is nothing new about blinkered reporting on China. Author Sterling Seagrave in his biography of the Empress Dowager Ci Xi described the tenor of China reporting at the end of the Qing Dynasty as follows:

> Little historical background was understood by westerners in China, who were dependent upon what they could learn from Treaty Port compradors or hired interpreters, who were themselves ill-informed and far from disinterested. Such people filled in the gaps in their knowledge with colourful inventions, because it was important to seem to know what was going on. Over drinks at the Long Bar in Shanghai or gossiping at the new racetrack, they mingled misinformation and supposition and passed it on by letter, diary, memoir, travelogue, diplomatic report, and journalism to the far corners of the earth, where it was accepted as fact.

To this day, much of what is accepted as fact about China in the Western press is derived in very much the same way. The Shanghai

Treaty Port atmosphere of speculation and hype described by Seagrave could very well be applied to Hong Kong where most journalists' China scoops originate. The analysis provided in the Western media is often flat, viewing China's political dynamics as a struggle between extreme factions (conservative-hardliner vs. liberal-reformist). Such extreme factions do not really exist. Deeper analysis of China's complicated politics has been left to academics and authors such as William H. Overholt, who wrote *China: The Next Economic Superpower*, and who has commented:

> For any historian of Chinese–American relations, the mystery is why the outside world failed to appreciate the positive aspects of China's course. Whereas any East European leadership that recorded one or two of China's achievements in 1994–95 would have been hailed for its genius, most of China's accomplishments attracted no attention in the Western press. As far as the average American could tell [from the media] China did little in this period except oppress its people and plan an invasion of Taiwan.

While there is nothing wrong with reporting negative events in China, to simply focus exclusively on them does not help Westerners coming to China, or their governments, to usefully comprehend those events and to place the economic, social, and political transitions occurring there today in their correct context. One observation which has been repeatedly made by Singapore's Senior Minister Lee Kuan Yew cannot be ignored in this regard. It is that the developed countries have a mutual vested interest in retarding China's economic growth for fear that China will become the next economic superpower, a new Japan of 1.3 billion people.

If one chooses to adopt Lee Kuan Yew's analysis, then it would seem (or at least the conclusion could be drawn) that the kind of statements which have become a predominant media trend have the effect of serving the political ends of countries wishing to contain China's economic growth and eventual coming of age as a world power.

MOTIVATIONS OF THE WEST

The Yuan Ming Yuan, the architectural wonder built by the Kang Xi and Qian Long Emperors, once stood as the epitome of Qing imperial splendour and refinement. It was a vast sequence of interlocking palaces with gardens and fairy-like pavilions, radiating outwards along crystal lakes covered with delicate bridges. The very existence of the Yuan Ming Yuan must have irritated European minds. Its splendour confirmed to the West that Europe has not attained the advanced level of culture that China had enjoyed for tens of centuries.

Today, when you stroll through the public park that was once Yuan Ming Yuan, in the suburbs of modern Beijing, you see nothing of this splendour—virtually everything that was Yuan Ming Yuan has been obliterated. The delicate palaces which once housed imperial treasures dating from every period of China's history are gone; only the stone foundations, which could not burn, remain to mark the pillar supports of the once-classic vermilion palaces and pavilions. The treasures once held within are today on display in the museums of those European countries whose forces sacked Yuan Ming Yuan.

Today, when you walk through the shattered remains, you can only ask yourself what kind of hatred could fuel such destruction.

In 1860, the British and French allied forces united in a single purpose: to cripple China politically and force it to open to the West—on Western terms—economically. The Emperor Hsien Feng had already fled to Chengde in the north, the old hunting lodge palace complex of the Qings. His dynamic brother, Prince Kung, became diplomat of the day. He kept the foreign forces at bay and refused to open the gates of Beijing to them. Unable to attack the political nerve centre of China, the allied forces attacked the cultural. Discovering the vast wealth outside Beijing's city walls, enshrined in the Yuan Ming Yuan and the Summer Palace, they broke into the palaces, stealing every conceivable item of value and destroying what they could not take with them. Pearls, jade, rubies and gold of immeasurable quantity and value were removed. Century-old vases were shattered, paintings of priceless value were indiscriminately burned, the precious Peking dogs—specially bred by the imperial household—were hurled head first into wells, and gold-embroidered dragon robes were heaped up and burned.

The entire complex of Yuan Ming Yuan and the Summer Palace was put to the torch. For weeks, the sky over Beijing was black with smoke. The destruction was vast, and intended to be complete. The statement was clear: precious items of immediate commercial value to China were to be taken by the foreign powers; precious items of cultural importance and value were to be destroyed completely.

In the weeks that followed, Prince Kung negotiated. The foreign powers wanted access to Beijing; they wanted the gates opened. Eventually, he was forced to acquiesce and the gates were opened. The foreigners entered; another treaty was signed. Trading ports which included Tianjin, Beijing, Nanjing and Guangzhou were opened, and foreign-occupied territories in China were put under foreign administration. Chinese law was not enforceable against foreign interests on Chinese soil in these foreign-administered enclaves.

The backdrop of these events cannot be forgotten or lost in understanding the dynamics of Chinese–Western relations today. It is not a question of old unsettled grievances, but the historical context upon which such relations have been established.

It is clear that the foreign powers did not have as their intention the toppling of the Qing imperial system. They chose not to attack the basis of the political nervous system of dynastic China. Rather, it was clearly their intention to have access and, moreover, control of China's resources. Leaving a weak political system in place was only to their advantage. Likewise, in another context, a strong Communist China with a heightened sense of nationalism has predictably posed more obstacles to foreign exploitation of China's resources than Chiang Kai-shek's Kuomintang, which was, historically, always malleable as far as money was concerned. Is it any wonder that American support and propaganda were for so many years (and even today) behind Taiwan and not China?

The elements of Western policy towards China at this critical period in history were to obtain unlimited access to China's market, that is, the selling of Western-manufactured finished goods to the vast Chinese population without restrictions or import duties; to have unlimited access to China's vast natural and/or crafted products at cheap labour costs; and to control trade. Foreign powers knew that a weak political system would have to tolerate their interests and commercial domination. In addition, foreign rights in China could not be touched by Chinese laws, foreign laws and administration were carried out within foreign enclaves, and complete diplomatic immunity was accorded to all foreign interests.

These elements have remained part of the collective unconscious underlying both the Western diplomatic initiatives today and the approaches of Western business interests in opening the China market. To a great extent, Western diplomatic relations with China are today driven by corporate interests seeking access to China's massive market potential as the most heavily populated country in the world (the fact that China accounts for nearly one quarter of the world's entire population is an awesome marketing statistic).

China's own regulations on foreign investment prohibit the creation of any kind of 'dependency' relationship. Foreign multinationals wishing to market their products in China must manufacture them in China, which requires investing there. This avoids a pure trade dependency relationship similar to that developed earlier between the developed West and Latin America or Africa. In a dependency relationship, finished goods from the industrialised countries are exported to underdeveloped countries in return for raw materials to be processed for export back to these developing markets. This has the spiral effect of keeping the underdeveloped world underdeveloped and concentrating capital in the developed world which grows ever richer through manufacturing finished products which the underdeveloped world becomes dependant on.

Being aware of the risks of dependency, China, like any other developing nation, views the promotion of 'American values' as an attempt to create dependency on American products. Should China become capable of producing its own products with its own technology at prices below those in America, then maybe Americans will find themselves dependant on Chinese-made goods. It is not totally unrealistic to foresee the day such an ironic situation actually happens.

China is driving forward on a policy of market economics which has created what is in fact becoming one of the most *laissez-faire* economies in the world today. The incredible materialistic drive of the Chinese people—a pent-up energy released by 15 years of reform—is gaining momentum of its own. China has come of age: this is a fact of our times. It cannot be denied by negative journalism, historic misunderstandings, misdirected animosities and emotions, or policies of 'containment'. The century beginning in the year 2000 will be China's.

PART I

POLICIES

我們要摸著石頭過河，
走一步，看一步。

When we cross the river,
we must first feel the rocks to make sure they are secure,
and then move forward taking one step at a time.

—Deng Xiaoping

CHAPTER 1

IDEOLOGY

革

Gé • Revolution

豹 變 爲 虎 之 課 。
改 舊 從 新 之 象 。

The image is a leopard being transformed to a tiger.
The symbol is to reform the old to the new.
—I CHING

易　經

I clearly remember, as a university student in America, the complete absence of courses teaching the basic premises of Marxism. While there was a plethora of courses on the different stages of America's 200-year history, and maybe one course on China's 4000-year history, there was nothing on Communism as such, or even Socialism, although—whether Americans liked it or not—these were the overriding political philosophies of most of the developing world at the time.

One day, a Japanese exchange student pointed out, 'You see, we in Japan practice a capitalist economy. Maybe Japan is the most capitalist economy in the world. But we don't always study capitalism. In fact, at university we spend much time and emphasis on learning about Marxism, about Communism.'

'But why study what the Commies are doing when Americans believe in capitalism?' retorted an American student.

'You cannot ignore these important philosophies,' responded the Japanese student. 'You must always learn from what others are practising. Failure to learn what others are practising, and to learn it well, will only lead to your own ultimate failure at what you are practising.'

MARXISM IN MODERN CHINA

Marx and Engels based their belief in communism's rise on the premises of Hegel's dialectic theory, which saw every historic development as a synthesis derived from the conflict between two opposing forces. Marx and Engels saw, in the conflicting forces of the class struggle resulting from exploitation in industrialised Europe, the eventual emergence of communism out of capitalism's decline. Lenin believed that this emergence could not passively evolve from the factors of natural decline, but instead had to be fomented through agitation. According to Lenin, the existence of opposing forces was not enough: communist revolution could only erupt from the concentration of carefully planned and directed energies. Where Lenin believed that only the industrialised cities could be ripe for agitation and eruption, Mao took revolution to the countryside, seeing the destitute rural masses as China's backbone for a new political mandate.

Regardless of whose theory held, the principles of Hegel remained constant. The foundation of each new interpretation of Marxism lay in the synthesis of a previous interpretation overlaid with the realities of the new situation. Marxist theoreticians, however, have the bad habit of getting too stuck on their own theories. Stiffness brings with it lifelessness. The eternal truth of Marxism lies not in its theoretical rigidity, but in its ability to be applied to ever-changing situations and adapted accordingly. Who is to say that the different theories or interpretations of Marxism as articulated by Che Guevara, Ho Chi Minh, Mao Zedong, Lenin or Marx himself were each in any way inferior to the other as long as their application to each individual circumstance worked?

Today, the Marxism of Deng Xiaoping, applied to a new set of conditions, forms the basis for not national revolution but rather industrial renovation. The theory remains the same; the application, and maybe the results, however, will be different. Likewise, the new synthesis is not between upper and lower classes, or urban and rural masses. The new synthesis is between the very principles of capitalism and communism. The catalyst of this synthesis will be a new kind of liberalised socialism, maybe better explained as market economics with paternal guidance. Hegel's dialectic itself was based on Darwin's notions of evolution—survival of the fittest. The China which is emerging at the end of the 1990s is a China which has survived more over the past century in the way of struggles, both internal and external, than have few other nations.

In pioneering a 'socialist market economy with Chinese characteristics', Deng Xiaoping at the close of this century has provided China with a catalyst for the next.

Rejection of the Soviet model

During China's wars of liberation—first against the Japanese and then the Kuomintang—China's Red Army had to develop its own theory of liberation based on the practical application of communist theory to China's own conditions. However, the dogmatic directives from Moscow being argued by Borodin, the '28½ Bolsheviks' (the pro-Soviet faction of the CCP, the Chinese Communist Party, following Mao's early opponent, Wang Ming) and other Russian advisors, insisted that the Chinese revolution be played out on the basis of Russian experiences drawn from the earlier theories developed by Marx. Mao Zedong and Deng Xiaoping were both strongly against the strict adoption of Soviet theories. The successive victories which brought Mao to power at the helm of the Chinese Communist Party during the Zunyi Conference of 1935 were won through the new application of strategies from the Chinese classics: Sun Tzu's *Art of War*, *The Romance of the Three Kingdoms*, the *36 Strategies*. In practical terms, Mao's political legitimacy was steeped in his profound understanding of China's past and his ability to apply lessons of the past to the present.

The China of the 1940s, however, was a China seeking to grasp the modern. Communism was the wave of the time because it spoke with clarity to virtually every non-Western country having undergone a colonial experience. Marxist theory explained the economic foundations upon which the Western world had compelled the non-Western into exploitation. Marxist explanations of the current status quo spread globally like a fever: China, Indo-China, Indonesia,

Malaysia, Africa and Latin America—each absorbed and reapplied the premises of Marxism to their own situation. In each case, Marxism provided a clear way forward, a common proposition— nationalist revolution.

In seeking a modern and international commonality to their revolution, Mao and his comrades were compelled to adopt the literature of communism as their own. Ironically, this was to a great extent driven by traditional Chinese values. For two millennia, Chinese learning had been based on memorising by rote the earlier classics. In the context of Chinese values, the modern revolution could not be rooted in a void. Therefore Mao, Zhou Enlai and Deng Xiaoping had to borrow the literature of Marx and Lenin to replace that of Confucious and Mencius. Following the liberation of Beijing, when Mao comfortably moved into the former imperial 'Sea Palaces' of Zhongnanhai, his enormous personal collection of Chinese classics was installed on the shelves of his study, where in the future he would receive foreign guests. It is said that his personal bodyguard, Wang Dongxing, was alarmed to find something missing amongst all these volumes. Wang quickly obtained copies of the works of Marx, Engels and Lenin which were strategically installed on the shelf where they were most likely to be seen by any guest sitting across from Mao.

The communists, however, were against rote memorisation of the Chinese classics, feeling that Chinese tradition hindered China's growth and that China should break with the traditions that required all action to be based on the classics. The desire to break with this tradition could be explained as one of the several theoretical bases of the Cultural Revolution. However, the tool—Maoism— which became the basis of overthrowing a collective philosophy of traditions with the intention of total liberalisation of thought, in turn became the framework which caged in Chinese thinking, only in a new context.

Legitimacy, power and the Spirit of Yanan

While, on the one hand, the Chinese Communist Party had created one of the world's most modern revolutions, serving as a panacea to the social ills of the time, this revolution was rooted in a society which remained largely traditional in its thinking. Despite the social transformation which the revolution brought with it, one cultural factor remained constant in the minds of the people: the legitimate basis of new ideas lay in old ideas. Only with such a link would the new ideas be accepted. Therefore, in a modern political context, China's leaders never directly present their views as their own. Rather, they will base the preposition of their ideas on those of their predecessor. In almost classic terms, both the Communist Party and the Kuomintang sought justification for their political existence on the back of the thinking and words of Sun Yat-sen (the universally accepted 'father of modern China').

Throughout Mao's life, and even after, his words and thoughts remained the basis of reference for all political actions and initiatives. Likewise, China's current leadership constantly refers back to Deng Xiaoping's ideas in their speeches and policy directives. Recent speeches by Jiang Zemin emphasising politics over economics are, in the interpretation of many Western analysts, signs of a 'reversal in Deng's policies'. These statements are really no more than assertions of Jiang's own newly consolidated power base.

Jiang can only follow in Deng's footsteps. He cannot depart from Deng's policies, much less reverse them. In this regard, it could be said that Jiang at this time does not yet have any clear policies distinctively his own. His legitimacy to serve as General Secretary of the Party derives from the fact that he is the best choice, compared to others. His selection was a compromise. By making reference to 'political work over economic', Jiang is grasping for legitimacy by dusting off old political mandates which he knows will not be disputed. In the Chinese collective unconscious, these may strike a chord with 'Maoisms'. By skipping back one era before Deng, Jiang is playing it safe. In time, when his own political legitimacy becomes unquestionable, Jiang may strike out with new and maybe even more liberal policies than Deng. But, before doing so, he must—like his predecessor—firmly root his legitimacy in things of the past.

Throughout Mao's career as helmsman of the People's Republic of China, each 'reform' initiative had (at least in his mind) its source in the thoughts which he espoused from his revolutionary base at Yanan. While Chiang Kai-shek secured himself in China's bastions of Western hedonism—the Opium Treaty ports of Shanghai and Nanjing—Mao the classic peasant revolutionary endured the harshness of Yanan. In Yanan, Mao pondered solutions to China's economic problems: a complicated feudal landholding system which had strangled production, Confucian values of hierarchy which guaranteed a stratified and stifling bureaucracy, and time-warped

family structures where women remained subservient and new generations were tied hopelessly to values of the past. Yanan became
Mao's proletarian 'Garden of Eden' where he lectured a new philosophy of political compassion and egalitarianism. He sought to create
a new society through the eradication of old values and feudal systems. No single philosophical forum had had as much influence in
terms of the number of people affected since the teachings of
Muhammad or of Jesus Christ, as did those heady days in Yanan.

Problems set in, however, following the liberation of China and
the ejection from the country of foreign colonialism, Japanese impe-
rialism and Kuomintang puppeteering. Amidst the rejoicing in
establishing the People's Republic, a new bureaucracy was established consisting of Mao's graduates from Yanan. With power, the
new bureaucracy grasped the prerogatives which came with power—
while Mao's philosophy had shattered the framework of tradition, it
had not altered tradition's behavioural patterns. Mao's gains in
achieving what amounted to a new nationalist social egalitarianism
were soon eroded by social stratification as the rising political elite
began to enjoy the taste of corruption in the form of privilege. Mao's
two critical political movements after 1949—the Great Leap Forward
and the Great Proletarian Cultural Revolution—became in turn
black marks on his record of achievements. However, both can be
viewed.from at least one perspective as representing attempts by Mao
to rectify the Party and bring the bureaucrats back in line with the
ideals of Yanan.

Mao's original intention was to drive China's development from
what was basically a mixed agricultural economy, with some specks of
industrialisation along the coast, into a fully industrialised socialist
economy without passing through any stages of development pre-
dicted as necessary by Marx. In more direct terms, Mao was trying to
catapult China into modernity without first navigating the country
through the stages necessary for economic maturity. Deng
Xiaoping's modification of Mao's ideas lay in recognising that conditions were in fact not ripe for the development of a pure socialist
economy. Deng believed, as a practical matter, that the country
needed to first move to the stage of a mixed market economy in the
form of a 'commodity economy' before China could consider developing itself along more socialist lines.

Mao wanted to not only abolish the commodity economy, but also
the monetary economy, in seeking to drive towards pure communist

egalitarianism. Mao considered his colleagues, Liu Shaoqi and Deng Xiaoping, too conservative in not adhering strictly to his ideals. Deng, the inevitable pragmatist, serving at that time as vice premier, was concerned with the problems of building a nation, and he wanted to solve them through experience gained on a case-by-case basis—not by adhering blindly to Marx, Lenin or even Mao's political theories. Mao wanted to force an ideal: Deng, recognising that either the ideal may not be attainable or that the results when attained may not be as good as expected, placed the ideal on an altar—something to be attained in the future but not now. Mao didn't want his ideals put on altars and not put into practice. On this point, Mao and Deng clashed. After Mao's death, and Deng's phoenix-like rise to power, Deng found that in fact he could not demolish Mao's ideals, as these had become the political justification for Deng's, and the Party's, own legitimacy in power. Deng could, however, keep these ideals for a future date and concentrate on the reality of what needed to be done at the moment.

THE RISE OF PRAGMATISM

On 13 January 1975, Zhou Enlai, body riddled with cancer, stood in the cavernous Great Hall of the People. For hours, he tirelessly delivered what was to be his last speech—the announcement to the world that China had adopted a new policy and a new road forward—the 'Four Modernisations'. Deng Xiaoping had already been hand-picked as Zhou's successor. Building on Zhou's 'Four Modernisations'—agriculture, industry, science–technology and national defence—Deng emphasised science and technology. Science and technology became the foundations for China's new future; Zhou's 'Four Modernisations' gave Deng the framework within which to work, the basis for going forward.

Where Mao had felt that human spirit and ideology could override scientific principles, which he viewed as 'Western' and therefore bourgeois in nature, Deng and Zhou's 'Four Modernisations' gave economic development full priority over political theory. Deng's socialism was a patient progression towards an objective while focusing on the economic problems at hand; Mao's was a zealous drive to achieve an ideal with complete disregard for the present problems, which had to be solved *en route*. Deng, like Mao, communicated his thoughts in rustic terms. Both men often advocated 'throwing out the afterbirth but keeping the child', selecting the good from the bad and throwing out the bad. In this respect, both men, in macro terms, saw eye-to-eye. Both emphasised the necessity of China going its own road. Mao insisted that China not adhere to the Soviet model; likewise, Deng stressed the need to not follow the models of America, Japan or even Taiwan, but rather develop a unique model based on China's own practical situations and actual experiences. Like building blocks, each experience became a step culminating in the construction of Deng's own independent framework in 1992, a 'socialist market economy with Chinese characteristics'.

'It does not matter whether the cat is white or black, it only matters if the cat can catch mice,' was, in fact, an old Sichuan saying going back years before Deng Xiaoping made it famous. Actually, it was Deng's comrade-in-arms and fellow field commander, 'one-eyed' Liu Bocheng who instilled this saying into Deng's mind. During their campaigns against the Kuomintang, when Trotskyite Wang Ming and the Soviet advisors preached their theories of conventional war to the Red Army, it was only too clear to Liu Bocheng and Deng that the communist forces would not be able to sustain a war on conventional terms against the Kuomintang's better equipped armies. In insisting that the advisors keep their theories and the Red Army fight a guerilla war, Liu Bocheng used the 'white–black cat' adage— war strategies meant nothing if they could not 'catch mice'. After Liberation, Liu Bocheng was appointed by Mao as one of China's '10 Marshals'. Deng appreciated Liu Bocheng's practical approach and made it his own. When China's economy floundered in the wake of the Great Leap Forward, Deng once again talked in 'white–black cat' terms.

Mao, however, wanted to go further. In reviving the spirit of Yanan, he sought to revive a spirit of self-sacrifice by all individuals for the greater good. The Great Leap Forward witnessed the communalisation of Chinese society, characterised by small production brigades and the inane melting down of everything made of metal in an attempt worthy of Don Quixote to industrialise China without laying down the infrastructure. On an individual level, the Great Leap Forward meant a complete distribution of assets and services, and an absolute end to private ownership of anything. Mao's Great Leap Forward echoed the egalitarianism of Yanan, when the communists were fighting a war and everyone was willing to make sacrifices. The

China of the 1950s, however, was developing. There was a spirit of rebuilding the nation, but, at the same time, people wanted the fruits of their labours and what they had fought for. Throughout the Great Leap Forward, slogans along the lines of 'Serve the People' echoed everywhere. Thirty years later, in the era of Deng reforms, the early entrepreneurs would justify their success by smugly saying 'I am "Serving the People". You see, I am a "People" too!'

It was the Liu Bocheng–Deng Xiaoping relationship which applied the 'white–black cat' adage to military tactics; another Liu–Deng relationship would apply 'white–black cat' tactics to economics. In seeking to reverse the damage done by the Great Leap Forward, then President Liu Shaoqi and Vice Premier Deng Xiaoping together exhorted the population to be pragmatic, as they ceased to advocate the selfless sacrifice which had undone China's economy, thus reversing the egalitarian policies of Mao. This step, however, also gave Liu and Deng the opportunity to advance themselves politically through advocating further pragmatic reforms. This was resisted by Mao who perceived it as a threat to his own overriding authority, which he insisted on maintaining regardless of actual results.

In the 1960s, China's Great Proletarian Cultural Revolution represented another attempt by Mao to revive egalitarian economics, on the one hand, while clearing the Party of privilege and complacency on the other. The communalisation drive was put into full gear, and cadres went to the countryside to learn from the peasants. In idealistic terms, it was Mao's last attempt to revive the spirit of Yanan. In cynical terms, by driving forward into pure communism, Mao was driving his political opponents out of power. Of course, Deng's 'white–black cat' comments became one of the first targets of the Gang of Four's attack. Mao's wife, Jiang Qing, used it as a tool to dislodge Deng from power: she called it 'revisionist thinking' and 'anti-revolutionary'. The ever-pragmatic Deng replied to her theoretic tantrums with characteristic disdain: 'Jiang Qing sits on the toilet all day but cannot shit'.

Deng lost power, but only for a while. With the Cultural Revolution having run its full cycle (leaving China's economy worse off than the Great Leap Forward), Mao had only one choice—bring the surviving pragmatists back. It was Premier Zhou Enlai who handpicked Deng to sit beside him as vice premier—and eventually as his successor. Deng's solution was simply to appeal to Chinese entrepreneurial instincts. In the wake of the Great Leap Forward, it had been his intention to revive agriculture by returning private farmlands to the farmers. As early as 1962, Deng had proposed returning land to peasants through a leasehold system which is adopted today. Under socialist principles, all land must belong to 'all the people', or the State. Deng's solution was to say that, while the individual could not own the land, he could own a 'right to use' the land, a right which was transferable, which, in practical terms, amounted to an effective right to the land itself. In this way, Deng was able to compromise theory in order to get results—while still upholding the theory. Tragically, however, it wasn't until 20 years later that Deng's post-Great Leap Forward approach was finally put into practice.

DENG'S PROGRESS TO THE TOP

It was not until the arrest of the Gang of Four (less than a month after Mao's death) that Deng received the green light that he needed. The turning-point would come during the Third Plenary Session of the Eleventh Central Party Congress in October 1978. However, Hua Guofeng, who Mao chose as his successor with the words, 'with you in charge I am at ease', was still in power. Hua Guofeng insisted that Mao's thinking not be changed or reversed, on the premise that this would make his position legitimate. Ironically, it became the tool with which Deng discredited Hua's adherence to theory and, with it, Hua's political mandate.

Like a military strategist in the field, Deng put into play the pieces that would lay the groundwork for his own rise to power. Turning to a trusted ally, Hu Yaobang, then the CCP's Head of Propaganda, an article discussing theory and practice appeared at Nankai University and was later published in the PLA's *Liberation Daily* under the protection of Deng who was then Vice Chairman of the Central Military Commission. Hu Yaobang courageously wanted the issues discussed in the article to be raised at the Eleventh Party Congress. This pulled the rug out from under Hua at the Congress and set the scene for Deng's rise to power. Out of loyalty, Deng ensured Hu Yaobang rose with him. The issues discussed became the basis of Deng's drive to remove political opposition and the foundation of his policies for development. Quoting Mao's saying, 'seek truth from facts', Deng argued pragmatism—to the extent that the saying is now more associated with him.

The Eleventh Party Congress marked the end of the Cultural Revolution, signified by a clear shift in focus from political internal struggle and ideological dogmatism to pragmatism and economic construction. The fall of the Gang of Four heralded a major change in power brokers, a capsizing of leftist ideologues in favour of more moderate pragmatists. Deng consolidated his power and control over China's Communist Party, government and military apparatus; from this point on the Party no longer based its programs for national development on pure political theory but turned instead to the development of law and rational economic and administrative systems. Deng rationalised this shift in focus along the lines of: 'If, on the one hand, you emphasise that "socialism is better than capitalism" but you don't have better conditions than capitalist countries, then it is obvious that theory doesn't work. Therefore the practical basis for theory is to have a socialist system that creates better conditions than under capitalism.' Deng's message was clear: 'Poverty is not socialism'. (A few years later, in building on Mao's own earlier but failed dream of raising China's living standards above those of England and America, Deng would shock the world: the paramount leader of the world's largest communist country said: 'To get rich is glorious'.)

The Eleventh Party Congress gave Deng carte blanche to implement the policy reforms he had master-minded some 20 years before. Two trusted deputies who had served in Deng's troops before Liberation, were hand-picked for the task ahead. Zhao Ziyang emerged as Party Secretary of Sichuan Province where he released the pent-up entrepreneurial energies of China's most populous province. Wan Li became Party Secretary of Anhui, where he concentrated on full-scale agricultural reforms aimed at clearing up the shambles left in the wake of the Cultural Revolution. By 1982, the people were saying, 'If you want to eat grain (*liang*) find Zhao Ziyang, if you want to eat rice (*mi*) find Wan Li' and both men had been raised to the Central Government, Zhao Ziyang taking over as Premier and Wan Li becoming Vice Premier under Zhao.

POLITICS AND ECONOMICS

The Thirteenth National Party Congress in 1987 marked another watershed in the construction of Deng's 'socialist market economy with Chinese characteristics'. Zhao Ziyang presided beside Deng, who noted that 'China had not yet reached the stage of communism . . . but had reached the stage of socialism . . . but this was only an initial stage of socialism . . . not yet advanced socialism'. Deng's conclusion was that while China must support socialism and develop it, China must at the same time develop according to the actual situation and 'not leap into socialism if we are not there yet . . . but develop step by step'. While the Eleventh Party Congress in 1978 recognised a commodity economy existing within the scope of China's planned economy, the Thirteenth Party Congress of 1987 recognised the commodity economy in its full existence coexisting beside a planned economy.

Zhao Ziyang, as Party General Secretary, announced clearly that 'class struggle' was no longer China's paramount problem, though he did recognise that class contradictions would always exist. The new direction, according to Zhao, was to eliminate class contradictions through economic development as opposed to political struggle. Economic development, however, carried with it costs, as inflation tied to growth reached unprecedented levels; workers' wages locked into the State enterprise system could not keep up with the inflation of the market. Zhao Ziyang said that this was a stage of development which everyone would have to bear for the benefit of future generations. 'Selflessness', however, had become a thing of the past in China.

In 1989, workers took to the streets to join the student protests against what was perceived as cadre bureaucratic nepotism and privilege—ironically, one of Mao's main themes in launching both the Great Leap Forward and the Cultural Revolution. Eventually, soldiers were called in to crush the protests. International shock from the sequence of events shattered investor confidence and China fell into two years of economic stagnation. The irony was that Zhao Ziyang, who had stood for so much in the way of economic reform for China, lost power as a direct result of the student action.

Getting results

In 1992, in a bid to revitalise the economy, Deng Xiaoping took an inspection trip south, an action very similar to Mao's own gestures of swimming across the Yangtse River before launching new political movements. At each stage of the trip, Deng visited the Special

Economic Zones (SEZs) which had been established under his experimental policies in the early 1980s. These were pockets of unrestrained *laissez-faire* dotting the coast, strategically positioned in Xiamen across the Straits from Taiwan, Zhuhai across from the Portuguese gambling den of Macao, and Shenzhen across from the epitome of *laissez-faire*, Hong Kong; two other SEZs, Shekou and Shantou, were near Hong Kong. In the late 1980s, Hainan Island was also declared an SEZ.

The controversial SEZ experiment which Deng pioneered in the 1980s had, by the 1990s, proved successful. The SEZs had become laboratories of economic explosion, vibrant industrial centres with a unique no-holds-barred gold rush atmosphere of their own. More importantly, they had become points of absorption and economic blending. Packed with Hong Kong, Macao and Taiwan cross-border investments, the SEZs had become more than models of growth— they represented the fusion of two systems.

Chen Yun, Mao's former Minister of Finance, who often supplemented Den's 'white–black cat' theory with his own 'bird cage' theory (the market should fly like a bird within the cage of State planning, but without a cage the bird will 'fly away') refused to visit the SEZs, labelling them 'capitalist'. Deng retorted that they were not capitalist because they were administered under China's Central Government, with Communist Party cadres serving as State officials monitoring and guiding the various stages of development. With long-time political ally, General Yang Shangkun, by his side, Deng spoke out throughout his travels in the south. 'Regardless of whether you call it capitalism or socialism, does it raise productivity?' Deng asked. Deng effectively eliminated labels—whether you call it capitalism or socialism or something else, the name is irrelevant. The whole point is that results are achieved from the policies applied and that those policies are aimed at achieving results.

Deng himself expressed disgust with Western extreme theories of liberalism which is his opinion were not actually put into practice. The apparent dichotomy fuelled Deng's own desire to modernise and pursue economic development in China without falling into what he saw as the confused state of mind of Western liberalism which had no clear direction in practical economic terms. In his view, political emotionalism must not interfere with China's development.

Western analysts often interpret China's experimental trial-by-error approach to economic reform as reform–reversal, new reform–new reversal; other interpretations see China's policies in terms of a two-steps-forward, one-step-backwards approach. Maybe the approach can be better described as feeling the way forward cautiously, taking the step boldly, and then making sure that the position is secure before taking another step.

Deng, on the one hand, exalted boldness in reform yet, on the other, he warned of careless haste. 'Cross the river by stepping carefully to assure the stones are in place,' he cautioned. 'No-one has gone this road before so we must go carefully . . . In crossing a stream we must be courageous in walking across the unknown . . . we must walk forward, we cannot walk back . . . but in taking each step we must be sure that it is the right step. So first feel the way and the stone to make sure it is secure before putting the weight on the stone.'

In combining socialist values with entrepreneurial freedom, Deng encouraged the people to 'grasp with both hands at the same time'. Using a symbolic left–right imagery, Deng spoke against the Chinese cultural tendency of moving from one extreme to another by preaching a middle road. On a more practical level, he warned against the extremes that could occur in a suddenly open economy, the abuse of opportunity at the expense of those socialist values that were beneficial to society collectively. Deng adopted Mao's axiom, 'seek truth from facts' as his own. However, his approach was to address specific economic needs and problems at the appropriate stage in China's development, which marked a decisive departure from the more sweeping and theoretical economic directives which marked the latter part of Mao's leadership.

The culmination of this progression in Deng's philosophy was the creation of a framework of pragmatism. Within this framework, China's entrepreneurial energies could be set free yet still kept within the bounds of a cautious approach to economic development.

A new economic model

With the collapse of the Soviet Union, some analysts predict that China will be next, based on the simplistic assumption that all communist systems are the same. Western press reports regularly air the notion that, by embracing capitalism, China is rolling back socialism and therefore communism in China will be undermined. Jumping to such conclusions completely misses the point of what is actually occurring in China today. Socialism is not dead, it is evolving. Just as it evolved from Marx to Lenin to Mao, it has been infused with new ideas to meet new situations, tempering theory with practice.

The socialism of modern China, moulded or still being moulded from the experimentation and fusion of socialist and capitalist mechanisms, represents a new economic model: it was always Deng's belief—as it had been Mao's—that China must follow its own path, borrowing selectively from other systems while retaining 'Chinese characteristics'. Notions that China for some reason must accept and adopt outright the systems of the West are anathema to China's leadership, reminding it of the days when Soviet advisors almost caused the Red Army to lose its campaigns against the Kuomintang.

Deng Xiaoping's thinking has unequivocally become Jiang Zemin's mandate of authority; in this regard, there can be no reversal of policies. The legitimacy factor aside, however, Deng has provided the framework for the development of China's economy into the twenty-first century, and a bridge between the revolutionary ideals of China's founders and the practical problems of today. It is essential, however, that one recognises Deng's framework as just that, a framework, on which, with Deng passing from active leadership, today's policies are being built. The current generation of leadership—Jiang Zemin, Li Peng, Zhu Rongji, Li Ruihuan, to name a few—has consciously refined Deng's framework to fit the rapidly accelerating changes which have come to characterise China's economy.

Does Deng's 'socialist market economy' mean a capitalist economy bearing a socialist flag to justify a theoretical link between the reality of China today and the zealousness of new China's revolutionary founders, or does it mean that China is in the process of selectively picking and choosing those aspects of socialism and those aspects of capitalism which in pure 'Dengist philosophy 'simply work'? One of the great ironies is that Deng recognised that socialism in its pure form does not exist in China and so pure socialism cannot form the basis of China's future. This is significant, especially as it contrasts sharply with politicians in Washington who fail to recognise that capitalism in its pure form does not exist in America at all—not only do they fail to recognise this fact, but they further fail to recognise that America today is more socialist in nature than capitalist.

At first impression, it might seem to Western analysts that the 'socialist market economy' is only a nomenclature for justifying China's departure from socialism and its adoption of capitalist tendencies. A more careful review of the situation reveals that the two systems function in a Yin–Yang balance, with market principles dominating in most sectors with State guidance, direction and even interference when a correction is required, while in limited sectors, State planning will still apply but only as necessary and only to complement the overriding energies of the market. This method of market management directs market energies rather than contain them. Like a t'ai chi master whose arm rests against his opponent's and moves with, as opposed to against, his opponent in taking negative force and redirecting it into positive force, so the intention is to create a kind of guiding apparatus of State macro-planning and macro-controls as opposed to a checks-and-balances approach as understood in the West.

When Deng described his vision for the future as 'a socialist market economy with Chinese characteristics', did the reference to 'Chinese characteristics' mean his philosophy of developing the 'socialist market' economy in line with the practical needs and realities of China and the Chinese people, or was it a way of providing the Chinese people with another carte blanche to take advantage of the 'anything goes' attitude they adopt when presented with opportunity? Maybe it is in the mystery of not knowing exactly what Deng actually meant that we find Deng's contribution to the future of China. Like Mao, who would recite a classic poem leaving its precise meaning to be interpreted by others, Deng has provided the building blocks for the next generation to work with. He has laid the foundations for the future of his country.

CHAPTER 2

POLITICS

晉

Jìn • Advancing

龍 劍 入 匣 之 課 。
以 臣 遇 君 之 象 。

The image is the dragon sword kept in its sheath.
The symbol is that one is finally presented with an opportunity to fulfil a goal.

—I CHING

易　經

The Chinese have a saying, 'The water and land of a place will be the source of nourishing the race of people that will emerge from that place' (*yi fang shui tu yang yi fang ren*). A country's geography, location and natural resources define and determine the conditions that prevail there. Development theory aside, the natural attributes of a country form the basis of its economic development; in the same way, its political system is based on economic, cultural and geographic factors. These three factors, and not political theory or ideology, form the real basis from which each system of government develops.

The government of the People's Republic of China must first consider the country's economic situation, cultural traditions and natural resources in determining its own direction and pace of development. This is a point which many Western governments overlook

in their relations with China, although without taking it into consideration, it is impossible to understand the basis of the Chinese
political system and body politic today. As one Chinese scholar
explained, 'China's cultural framework has developed on the earth
of China, not in America, France or other countries'.

PROBLEMS OF SCALE

China's political system has developed from China's history and 5000
years of unbroken cultural development. During this period, the
geographic land which is China, even when ruled by a people from
beyond the Great Wall (Mongolians during the Yuan Dynasty and
the Manchurians during the Qing), has consistently been developed
under the cultural dominance of the Han (Chinese) people, with
other minorities partly involved.

Under the weight of 5000 years of history, cultural values and
social behaviour in modern China cannot be lightly changed,
although since commencing its economic reforms, Western culture
has come to China in large doses. However, Chinese culture has consistently remained the overriding force and continues to influence
the Chinese people's thinking—a basic and essential factor to consider when developing a body politic. China has always been large in
scale, at least from the Tang Dynasty through to the Qing Dynasty,
during which time its borders remained more or less constant. From
the Yuan Dynasty, when Marco Polo visited the Great Khan, through
to the Qing Dynasty when the British came to buy silk and tea,
China's culture and politics served as major influences on Western
culture.

Today, China is one of the largest countries in the world—it is cer-
tainly the most populated. There are too many people: as one
Chinese banker noted in a sweeping yet perceptive statement, 'All of
our problems arise from the population problem. This is what makes
us in China different.' The proportion of natural resources to
people is, in fact, relatively small. China's landscape is dominated by
mountains and deserts, and naturally irrigated and arable areas are
few. At the same time, China is aiming to become one of the world's
most developed countries, which will demand both industrial expansion and agricultural efficiency. In order to achieve this objective,
China still has a long road ahead of it; it will require constant and

careful planning to maximise, without destroying, the few (proportionate to population) natural resources China has.

FOREIGN RELATIONS

Many countries are afraid of China. Because they do not understand the geographic limitations and historical development of China, they are afraid it will develop too quickly and that China's political system will influence Western systems. This fear has no practical basis when one looks at the problems of population control and resource management which the leadership must handle as a first priority— at least for the next few decades. It is unfortunate that Western perceptions of China's political system are still steeped in the images of China's Cultural Revolution—masses draped in grey waving red books at a stoic Mao atop of Tiananmen—with power generating from a single leader. This view is reinforced by a dim understanding of communism and comparisons between the Mao of generations past and other dynamic leaders, such as Kim Il Sung of North Korea and Fidel Castro of Cuba, and results from a failure to look closely at the factors that are unique to China's own political system. America, for example, has never been able to clearly separate Chinese and Russian communism.

Westerners still remain naive concerning the development of communism in Asia. They view the philosophy as singular, monolithic and not empirical. They fail to see that some current institutions in the West are more socialist in nature than those in China, although it claims to be socialist. In fact, in some sectors there is far more free-wheeling freedom in China in the pure sense of free market economies than exists in many Western so-called capitalist countries. There is a dangerous gap in knowledge about one of the world's most competitive trading partners and potentially most powerful economy.

America's embargo

China's long years of economic and political isolation between 1949–79 represented a political imposition—none of the economic embargoes (those placed against Cuba, Vietnam and Cambodia) lasted as long, as had such an effect in real terms, as the embargo placed against China by the United States. America's isolation of

China coincided with its continued support for Chiang Kai-shek's regime, which America insisted upon believing held political ideals similar to its own. There is little debate over the historical facts surrounding Chiang Kai-shek's regime: corrupt to the core, intertwined with the Shanghai 'Green Gang' mafia, suppressive and totalitarian. Nevertheless, America insisted on recognising this regime as 'Free China', even after it was popularly expelled from the mainland.

Washington determined that Chiang's regime be recognised and Mao's isolated. Reports from journalists in the field, such as Edgar Snow and Theodore White, were often not published, as editors felt compelled to reflect the views of the anti-communist right wing of Washington. Nobody in Washington really tried to understand what communism was for 'New China', or the ideals driving the new leadership and the problems confronting it as it sought to unify and reconstruct the nation. In this regard, Washington's policy towards China, in broad terms, has not changed all that much over the past 40 years. Following the strong reception given to Lee Teng-hui by a number of US senators and congressmen during his visit to New York in 1995, it is clear that the predominant thinking of America's right-dominated Congress is, at least in terms of China, still locked in the mind-set of the 1950s and 1960s.

Soviet intentions

Having thrown out the Soviet advisors following the Zunyi Conference in January 1935, Mao remained concerned with the possibility of Soviet dominance over China's political and economic spheres. In the simplest of *realpolitik* terms, China shares a 4000-kilometre-long border with Russia. Historic confrontations, and border claims in Manchuria and Xinjiang, were reason for concern. Soviet dominance of the newly independent country of Mongolia was a compromise, to allow a weak buffer state to absorb the potentially oppressive policies of the Soviet Union on China's northern border.

Soviet insistence that China adopt political, military, and economic lines of thinking—which were developed for social and economic conditions in the Soviet Union, but not applicable to those conditions in China—posed a clear conflict of interest. Russia, historically, was also one of the European countries to obtain territorial concessions in China following the Opium Wars, and this precedent in itself was a basis for concern over future intentions.

In 1958, the Soviet Ambassador to China, Yudin, paid a visit to Mao Zedong, placing a proposal on the table. Its chief terms were that the Soviet Union would build a navy for China; it would be a cooperative navy using Russian ships in all of China's ports; the navy would be run by the Soviet Union; and, while Chinese would be able to man some of the ships, overall operations would be under the command of a Soviet-appointed admiral. Mao asked Yudin to repeat the proposal again so as to make sure that there was no misunderstanding. Mao then replied: 'We know Russia doesn't have any warm-water ports; that is what Russia has wanted since the time of Peter the Great. Now it appears that we should give you control of all the ports we have. OK. After that, I will go up into the mountains and lead our guerillas against you.'

Following Liberation in 1949, China's relationship with the Soviet Union was an uneasy continuation of relations rather than an alliance. Mao himself wished to see China align with the United States and establish relations with this less immediate threat; failure by the United States to recognise China made this impossible. In fact, it took an established right-wing conservative president, Richard Nixon, to initiate relations with China against overwhelming anti-communist sentiment in America. A similar initiative by a more liberal politician would have carried with it too great a political cost at home.

The Collective Approach

China's is not a political system built around a single individual; it is and has always been a collective system. The collective decision-making that supports the Chinese system is a cultural factor unique to China. Historically, the founder of a dynasty would be a military strongman who, to consolidate his grip on power, became a political leader. Generations of emperors, however, found their lives ruled as much by court etiquette as by the role they played as the pivot around which the powerful political and military clans revolved. Modern China can only depart so far from its past. Regardless of whether the legal apparatus adopted for China's political system is imperial and headed by an emperor, or communist and headed by a chairman, it is still fundamentally collective.

China's collective approach to government is rooted in tradition.

The main priority of each Chinese leader is not to appeal to notions of democratic rule *per se*, but rather to rule effectively and raise the people's standard of living; the focus is upon results, not upon theoretical procedure. To this end, the collective views of others must be sought at each level of government or popular administration. That is to say, the collective approach has grown upwards from the village level, where traditionally village elders had to seek consensus of opinion when decision-making. Such an approach, in a more modern context, lends itself to the rural, district, and urban committees which make up the framework of socialist government at the grassroots level. Likewise, the decision-making at the Central Party or Government level consists of the consolidation of various opinions from the leaders in Zhongnanhai (the Party Central Committee and State Council headquarters in Beijing), as opposed to seeking a simple majority in the face of polemic views.

The logical outcome of the collective decision-making process is a decision or result that everybody is able to live with, to one degree or another. Equally important, everybody is involved in this decision and therefore is capable and willing to implement it—or to take responsibility. It is hard to envisage a situation where the PRC Government's annual budget could, like America's in early 1996, be frozen between rival factions of government debating contentious issues in an election year. In China, the business of government is getting on with it.

From emperor to chairman

In the traditionalist view of the Chinese people, the effective leader is a person who is able to seek views from all different opinions: 'Listen to all different views, and your decisions will be correct' is a traditional saying. The emperor of China was idealistically always 'correct' in the minds of the people. The rationale, however, was not because the emperor himself was a brilliant decision-maker, but that the emperor was able to draw on a plethora of advisors who could present a whole range of views from which he could make a decision that was acceptable to all.

In imperial times, the emperor was a symbol of the nation and national unity. Historically, however, there were very few emperors who could act in an entirely autocratic manner. The first, Emperor Qin Shi-Huangdi, ruled with an iron fist. In subsequent dynasties, the founder of the dynasty rose to power through military prowess, and had all the characteristics of a war-lord strong man, although his rise to military authority was almost always due to competent advisors from whom he could seek direction. However, as power passed from generation to generation, the emperor became more the focal point of a general bureaucracy which functioned as a government unto itself, with the emperor serving as a symbolic and often ceremonial head of state rather than as a dictator (as is so often the simplified view portrayed in Western versions of Chinese history).

The factions which existed in the Chinese body politic—whether military, regional, commercial or family—and the continual compromises between them were often the most important part of keeping the empire together. Lobbying, or rather seeking the views of each faction in the interests of unity, has always been the basis of decision-making for the traditional body politic in China—from village to imperial household. Likewise, collective decision-making has remained the salient feature of the communist body politic. The 'spirit of Yanan' is depicted as a triumvirate, with Mao in the centre, Zhu De heading the Red Army and Zhou Enlai in charge of government affairs. The image is one of cohesion at times of stress.

Even at the height of his power, Mao Zedong relied on the support of the Central Government as well as that of regional leaders. Mao's famous train rides across China, visiting regional Party leaders prior to initiating political campaigns, were a part of the collective process. Decision-making has since been characterised by consultation between the various departments and power brokers in China.

The centralisation of power

From the Great Leap Forward in the 1950s to the end of the Cultural Revolution in 1976, political struggles at the top took their toll, leading to a gradual decrease in the number of capable leaders, and power became centralised to the point of political myopia. There was no separation of power (needless to say, balance) between the Party, government, military, judicial and administrative institutions, and they merged into a single, central chaotic force, headed by the Politburo. This was largely being driven by the Gang of Four, whose initiatives were only kept in check by Mao, who was Chairman of the Party. During these years, the distinction between Party and Government ceased to exist.

With the passing of Mao in 1976, power slid into the hands of his ambitious, psychotic wife and her three youngish followers, Zhang Qunqiao, Yao Wenyan and Wang Hong Wen, known to the world as the Gang of Four. The country slipped into further disarray as they moved to consolidate their power.

Following the coup against the Gang of Four in 1976, less than a month after Mao died, a three-year restructuring of political power accompanied the phoenix-like ascendancy of Deng Xiaoping. Deng's mandate was confirmed at the Eleventh Party Congress in 1978, when the open door policy was crystallised. From the time he took power, Deng (who himself was a victim of centralised personality-based politics) consistently stressed the necessity for political reform to occur in parallel with economic reform; that is, the decentralisation of government combined with the building of legitimate institutions. It has always been Deng's aim to break down the past patron–client personality politics of the country in favour of clearly established government institutions working according to organised reporting systems and procedures clearly defined by law.

One may look at history and say that Deng Xiaoping himself, however, was a master at orchestrating personality politics and the patron–client relationships which have come to characterise his epoch of political dominance. At the same time, if one looks at the changes within the government system that have occurred since Deng's rise to power, one can only acknowledge that such changes have been momentous in terms of extent of organisation, channels of procedure, and rule by law as a basis for development.

Personality politics

In imperial China, the executive and judicial functions were fused. So, when the Communist Party with Mao as Chairman came to power in 1949, they inherited a tradition where political power was the source of law. Just as imperial households had done before, they put in place an elaborate bureaucratic system with the power base at the centre. For Mao and the early revolutionary leaders who were born in the shadows of the Qing Dynasty, it was one thing to create a new system of government; it was, however quite another to depart completely from a traditional collective system of government that the Chinese people had known for 4000 years.

Prior to 1979, there was essentially a conflict between Party and

Government, with the Party clearly overriding Government authority. However, in the natural course of leadership transfer, the seemingly one-man grip which Mao once held over the Government through his position as Party Chairman became diffused. Deng's own grip on power was limited by the fact that his faction had to rely on the support of others to survive, and it is due to this fact that a more consultative governing process has evolved.

The next generation of leadership, that surrounding Jiang Zemin, lacks the charisma of Deng's generation, leaving a situation in which personality politics come second to collective government systems. This in itself has led to the strengthening of government institutions, as it is obvious that, with this generation, no single individual has the strength of personality—or the revolutionary credibility—to dominate and successfully implement policy in the game of personality politics.

The new leadership

Today, the power structure in China is more collective and balanced than at any time since the heady days of Yanan. It is clear that the economy and the administrative apparatus of government is divided among and managed by the power groupings around Jiang Zemin: Zhu Rongji is the dynamic financial reform wizard, Qiao Shi has years of experience in the internal Communist Party intelligence apparatus, and Li Ruihuan devised the development program that rebuilt Tianjin. Jiang has also forged a deep alliance with Li Peng, the adopted son of Zhou Enlai, giving Jiang's administration credibility through continuity with the original revolutionary ideals of modern China's founders.

In another context, we could see Chairman Jiang Zemin as a kind of modern Liu Bei of the Three Kingdoms Period, AD 220–265. While Jiang himself does not stand out as having a distinctive character, he has managed to surround himself with a number of brilliant leaders, such has Zhu Rongji. Another Zhu—Zhu Geliang of the Three Kingdoms Period—was also such an advisor. While Zhu Geliang, a near-legendary strategist, never held the position of emperor, he is regarded by all Chinese people with a degree of respect accorded few emperors in China's history. This illustrates the respect the Chinese people have for the emperor's counsellors, and for the collective decision-making inherent in central government rule.

The magic behind the lesson of Zhu Geliang was that Liu Bei, who was the King of Shu during the Three Kingdoms period, selected Zhu Geliang as his advisor. Liu Bei himself was not regarded as a superior thinker; however, through his careful selection and management of advisors, he was able to make the correct strategic decisions leading to the successful establishment of his kingdom. When Jiang Zemin and Zhu Rongji are viewed together (the former Party Secretary and Mayor of Shanghai respectively) in the context of China's collective governing process, we could see the emergence of a modern Liu Bei and Zhu Geliang relationship.

Political reform and decision-making

Collective consultation underpins every decision-making process in China today. Using the legislative process as an example, when a law is drafted, each department concerned will be involved in the drafting process, adding its opinions. Session after session of drafting and reviews will take place so that the final product is a reflection of the various ideas of all departments affected by this law or involved in its implementation.

This entire concept is in stark contrast to American-style democracy, which bases all decision-making on the power of a simple majority. This lack of consensus in the American system is difficult for the Chinese to grasp: from their point of view, if 51% agree on one issue, or on the selection of one political candidate, why should 49% suffer?

American democracy can be broadly defined as consisting of two political parties: the Democrats and the Republicans. In the view of most Americans, the Democrats represent the liberal party (left) and the Republicans the conservative (right). If one looks at the situation from China's point of view, it would seem that there is only one totalitarian party in America, with two factions: the Democratic faction, which is right of centre in its conservatism, and the Republican faction, which is extreme right of centre in its ultra-conservatism. Attempts to introduce other parties appear to have been unsuccessful. The existence of a communist party is in fact prohibited (though perhaps not under law). Suggestions by America that 'China should have political reform along with economic reform' are seen by the Chinese as an attempt to directly interfere in the logical growth and development of another country's political system. What makes such interference even more distasteful to the Chinese is that it is based on ill-informed sources, or more precisely a lack of knowledge about the political reforms that have already taken place within a remarkably short period of time in China. Furthermore, the American view is based upon a political framework that developed in America over a 200-year period to meet the needs of the American people. Such a system would fail miserably if introduced in China, given China's unique circumstances and political history.

Political reform in China cannot be seen in such simple terms as the development of a one-man, one-vote democracy. Firstly, this approach is irrelevant when China's own traditions of government, which have always demanded strong centralism, are considered. Secondly, the political reforms that are taking place in China address different issues altogether, issues that are far more relevant to the transition China is undergoing today.

Returning first to the strong centralism that characterises China's traditional system of government, this derives from the traditional emperor's 'right' to rule, a 'mandate' from heaven. In modern terms, the chaos of the disintegration of Kuomintang rule, in the minds of China's rural masses, effectively gave this traditional mandate to the Communist Party. The ability of the Party to retain power depends upon its ability to fuse economic progress with an ethos representing its symbolic mandate—this means upholding the banner of Chinese nationalism, which in itself provides a spiritual legitimacy to rule, while raising economic conditions generally and the standard of living of the people specifically.

This concept, rooted in the Chinese people's 4000-year collective unconscious, falls on stony ground in the West; as the conditions under which this collective unconscious evolved have never really existed in the West, the West has no way of understanding the conditions under which effective and successful government in China can be carried out. If Chinese peasants were given a direct right to vote for the nation's leadership, they would scarcely understand why they had been so selected. The act of providing this voting option could only be interpreted to mean that the current leadership no longer had a 'mandate' to rule. The very idea of organising voting primaries, in the minds of the rural and working masses, could only be tantamount to chaos (*dao luan*): tradition holds that only in circumstances of dire chaos can the mandate of rule be transferred legitimately. Simply put, Western notions of building American-style 'democratic' institutions in China are irrelevant to China and would result in nothing but chaos.

Americans watch political conventions every four years on their televisions and point to these New Years Eve party-like scenes with trumpets, paper hats, signs and lots of noise as democracy in action—the people's right to rule. Chinese watching such hysteria are just dumbfounded. In the Chinese mind, such events are more like chaos than constructive government. The system just wouldn't work in China.

The impetus for China's political reforms began with Deng Xiaoping. These reforms are aimed at addressing certain issues facing China today which are very real. Attempts are being made to coordinate the relationship between Party and Government and determine the appropriate areas in which the authority of one should take precedence over the other; to recategorise the authority and specific roles to be played by and between the National Party Congress and the National People's Congress in parallel with the role of political policy versus statutory law; to seek an appropriate balance between Party policy directives and legal procedures in the judicial arena; to find a balance of power and delineate authority between the Central and local government levels; and to restructure the relationship between Government and State-owned enterprises.

From the Party's point of view, some reforms are still being carried out. These reforms involve changing its function from that of government to the formation of ideological parameters and policy platforms; not getting involved in specific government tasks, which have now been transferred to the government and the judiciary; and having the Party consider policy issues from a macro-perspective and not engaging in administrative and government work.

From the Government's point of view, reforms still being implemented will give greater independent decision-making and self-reliance to State-owned enterprises, focus more on policy decision-making and less on bureaucratic detail, and change the previous pattern of making direct investments and governing business too directly. The Government will refrain from trying to control markets, prices and commercial decision-making, and focus on allowing the economy to flourish on free-market terms with limited policy parameters and intervention only when necessary.

Simultaneously, cadre and political personnel functions have undergone change. Today, regardless of who is in power, the bureaucracy or administrative system will remain intact to provide continuity regardless of change in policy.

The selection of people is now carried out through an election system, albeit with limitations. Regardless of the current limitations, the clear direction is to gradually develop this system; there is also a clear policy on the retirement of officials, to prevent a concentration of power in the hands of an elderly elite for too long a period, as happened in the past.

POLITICAL DEVELOPMENT IN CHINA

It is clear that China's system cannot be exactly like a Western system— the cultural, historical, social and economic factors in China are simply not the same. While the leadership recognises a need to absorb Western principles which have proved to be effective in other countries, and adapt them to China's own specific needs, China cannot entirely copy another system. The leadership will still be leadership under the Party, it being the strongest leadership group in China.

What the Chinese people fear most is political unrest. China has known its greatest periods of peace under a strong central leadership such as during the Tang and Ming dynasties. Most Chinese in China today actually recognise the necessity for maintaining a consistently strong Party leadership: chaos does not benefit anyone, therefore change must come gradually, step by step.

China does not want a Western model of 'true' democracy when it observes some countries, such as those of Latin America, where numerous parties are in constant struggle and have no unity of direction. From China's perspective, whether there are many parties or one party, if the people can put forward their views and participate in political decision-making in a practical way (through the Party, local committees, etc.) that too represents the spirit of democracy. China believes that democracy is unanimity, the collective pursuit of ideas and the achievement of targets that have been selected through a process of internal consultation, not an external conflict where 49% of the population must endure the decision of the other 51%. China is not a culture of black and white, but a culture of Yin and Yang.

China's fears of Western democracy, therefore, are based on a fear of chaotic small parties fighting among each other for a voice, leaving the country without a direction; a wish to avoid the unnecessary factionalism which erupted during previous attempts to adopt a Western-style government during the Republican period; fear of ending up with a government unable to make decisions because it is paralysed by interest groups (the American budget freeze of 1996 provides an example of exactly what China does not want and cannot afford to have); and a concern that democracy applied to China could result in uneven growth throughout the country, which could have negative effects in terms of labour unrest, social unrest, and the distribution of commodities.

Democracy, the result of which was 'pure' democracy in the Cultural Revolution, resulted in factionalism. Factionalism is what happens in China when there is a power vacuum. War-lords predated communism, in the 1920s and 1930s, and were the result of Western democracy as introduced by Sun Yat-sen, a separation of powers among government, judiciary and party along Western lines of authority. The Cultural Revolution, however, only resulted in a messy merging of party/military security and government functions.

Today, political developments in China are moving towards a more formal balance of power between official bodies. This involves a clear strengthening of the role of the National People's Congress. Once criticised by Western analysts as being a 'rubber stamp' for the Party, it has developed over recent years, asserting its role as national parliament, formulator and passer of laws. In turn, the Party and Government are both moving towards a more legally based and systematic structure: the development of a complete and effective legal system is a matter of priority and a pre-condition to developing a higher level democracy.

The role of the judiciary has also been strengthened and the implementation of law has become more systematic and procedural. In March 1996, the National People's Congress adopted new legislation providing protection for individuals in criminal prosecutions, including rights to legal defence and protection against detention without adequate cause.

THE POWER STRUCTURE AFTER DENG

Mao said that 'political power comes down the barrel of a gun'. Mao's view was that the Party must control the gun, not the gun control the Party. The question which does remain unclear is the effect that Deng's death will have upon the military. The military has always remained a crucial force in China's political equation. At the present time, the visible leadership, under Jiang Zemin (who holds the posts of General Secretary of the Communist Party, Chairman of the Central Military Commission, and Chairman of the State), is supported with Deng's blessing.

Although Chairman of the Central Military Commission, a body of China's top commanding generals, Jiang himself has no actual military experience. In this respect, many outsiders speculate that he has no real patron–client support network in the military, and without Deng's blessing, his grip would be tenuous at best. Jiang, nevertheless, in the style of a modern Liu Bei, has carefully promoted a number of generals loyal to him to their current positions in the military hierarchy. This has included the appointment of Generals Zhang Wannian and Chi Haotian as Vice Chairmen of the Central Military Commission, which was formerly dominated by Deng's own appointees.

Just as Deng Xiaoping introduced a program of accelerated retirement to shift sideways old die-hard revolutionaries who represented a block to his own reforms (and eventually got them off the stage altogether), Jiang has similarly introduced a program of accelerated promotion within the military. A whole fresh crop of generals has been promoted to senior ranks under Jiang's leadership to create a new tier of loyalty, while Jiang has gradually retired a number of stalwarts closer to Deng. While a key move in ensuring Jiang's political survival, such measures are, of course, not an absolute guarantee of power. However, the military remains a key factor in gaining support for the leadership and whatever platform it puts forward for China's reforms and development. In this regard, the military would be unlikely to exert its force in a coup, as is often the pattern in other developing countries—it would take an extreme situation in China to trigger such an event.

The Pentagon report

Western analysts worry over 'What will happen when Deng Xiaoping dies?' However, this is not an issue for the average Chinese, who sees the current collective leadership as the future power structure, and Deng Xiaoping as a historic symbol who, as a leader, has already passed from effective power.

A declassified US Government Defense Department report was released to the press during the week of 22 January 1995. After making some general assumptions concerning China's economy and political situation, it arrived at a number of surprising conclusions. These included assertions that '. . . there was a 50–50 chance that China would disintegrate under a post-Deng diffused leadership and internal conflict. Power in general will gravitate away from the centre'; that 'China is up for grabs once Deng passes away. There is no apparent balance of political forces and Deng's death will create a political vacuum for both conservatives and reformers to move in', and that there is likely to be a return to 'hardline repression'.

The report also states that, 'China is the major uncertainty in Asia's future' and envisions a militaristic China emerging in the region. It predicts China forcibly retaking Taiwan, and 'Triad groups emerging as the dominant leadership in Asia'. It reads something like a popular action novel. The '50–50' scenario was based on a reflection of personal views from a panel of American sinologists who were asked their opinion. The panel consisted of some 15–20 American academics and one Pentagon official. Given that the panel consisted largely of academics from American universities, one might ask the extent to which these panellists had been in touch with actual political events and economic change in China over the past five years (1991–96 have marked probably the greatest period of change in modern China since the Communist Party's ascendancy to power in 1949).

The view that 'China is up for grabs' is irrational, as the country is clearly moving forward in accordance with a fairly unified reform policy. While there are problems with Central Government control over the regions, and difficulties in implementing reform policies at the local level, this is the cost of shifting away from a centralised State-planned economy to one driven by market initiatives. The fact that the panellists, whose input was the main source of information for the Pentagon report, could not name any clear potential leadership in China is probably more a reflection of their lack of knowledge of the current situation than a reflection of the state of China's leadership.

A leadership of reformers

The Pentagon report is full of irresponsible analysis based on uninformed assumptions. For instance, the statement, 'Deng's death will create a political vacuum for both conservatives and reformers to move in', demonstrates that the panellists are completely out of touch with the current political scene in China (something which is not surprising given that most are limited to reading books about China in their respective university libraries).

Currently, there is no 'conservative' versus 'reformer' conflict in China; basically everyone in the central leadership and the military is a 'reformer'. Political viewpoints, of course, differ between the various groups, but the basic dynamic of reform is the clear policy throughout the Government today. Periodic adjustments in lending and credit policy, foreign exchange, trade liberalisation and enterprise reform are features of monitoring and adjusting a transitional economy, not reflections of any power struggle between polemic forces. Likewise, a return to 'hardline repression' is something of the past. China has clearly moved on from the situation that existed during the 1960s and 1970s, despite the fact that the Western media continue to characterise China as it was during those years. A mere trip to Shanghai will clear anyone's mind of such illusions. Furthermore, parts of the report which predict a Chinese invasion of Taiwan, or an ascendancy of triad rule in Asia, are reflections of fantasy and an overdose of popular news-stand novels. If anyone wants to see what happens in the world of real 'Mafia-politics' all they need do is take a trip to Las Vegas.

It might be worth noting that this particular Pentagon report was declassified right in the middle of sensitive US–China trade negotiations over intellectual property issues. The timing of this cannot be ignored in assessing whether the report was meant to serve as a correct reflection of China's state of affairs or as a form of anti-China propaganda, a political negotiating tool and a form of muscle-flexing during a period of critical bilateral trade negotiations. In its claim that, following Deng Xiaoping's death, China would have a power struggle for succession and would split into civil war throughout the various military regions, the report seems to reflect what the American government would like to see rather than the actual situation in China.

In fact, the question of Deng's death is almost irrelevant in the minds of most Chinese citizens. Deng has long passed from the scene of active political power. The strong-man personality has given way to a Government which is more a collective body around Jiang Zemin, a system of factional checks and balances. At the moment, it seems unlikely that any single personality force or political faction can by itself out-manoeuvre the others as all depend on each other for continued support in the scenario of today's China.

CHAPTER 3

HUMANISM

履

Lǚ • Stepping

如 履 虎 尾 之 課 。
安 中 防 危 之 象 。

The image is trampling on the tail of a tiger.
The symbol is of keeping prepared for possible future perils while enjoying peace.

—I CHING

易 經

The classic Chinese novel 'Dream of the Red Chamber' has one famous line: 'The bigger it is, the bigger the problems' (*da you da de nan chu*). China's big problem is China's population; there are just too many people. This is a problem which is a very real one and which must be addressed in practical terms—theory and ideals do not always solve real problems.

China's people must live and eat, the children need education, the older people need social benefits, the young and middle-aged need work. The Government of the People's Republic of China must provide all of this: food, staples, housing, education, employment, every kind of social insurance and welfare, hospitals and healthy working environments. The provision of all these things must be considered from the perspective not only of China's bustling cities and exploding economic coastal regions, but from the perspective of China's rural masses, minority regions, underdeveloped backwaters, mountain ranges and deserts, which constitute a great part of the geographical mass that is China. China must consider the disparity between eastern and western regions, urban and rural. Regardless of where people are born, in all areas of China they have the right to exist.

According to international law, the question of human rights may be viewed on two planes: a person's right to exist, and a person's right to develop. A person's right to exist is a basic right: a person's right to develop is a question of conditions and an individual's attitude when living under these conditions. For China, the human rights question is a question of 1.3 billion people having a right to eat. Is it little surprise that the Government gives top priority, under the new Five-Year Plan, to agricultural development? China must achieve agricultural self-sufficiency before it can begin to address the question of human rights. Only when the question of simple human existence has been resolved—when all have food—can people begin to prosper. Until this basic condition of existing is met, one can never begin to discuss the right to develop in any way that will be meaningful to 1.3 billion people.

The West's preoccupation with human rights as a political issue has always been focused on the right to develop. Examples include the right of minority groups to have equal opportunities, equal rights for races and sexes at the workplace, and social recognition of gays. A poor country like China can only approach these issues on a step-by-step basis. One cannot take the conditions that exist in China and compare and judge them with the conditions existing in already developed countries.

From China's point of view, no government can be expected to address the question of personal development rights if it cannot first guarantee its people's existence. If China tried to focus on the issue of personal development rather than the issue of existence at this early stage of its economic development, it would result in nothing but chaos (*tian xia da luan*)—literally, 'All under heaven is chaos'. The result would be that even the very basic right to exist would be placed in jeopardy. However, efforts are being made in China to address the right to develop—some of these efforts are quite new. Therefore progress in this regard, and the speed of that progress, cannot be judged against the efforts of more developed countries which have had a longer period in which to grapple with these problems from both a social and economic perspective. In the West, starvation, as a fact of life, has for the past 200 years more or less ceased to be a problem; the same cannot be said for China.

THE GROUP, NOT THE INDIVIDUAL

In China, the concept of human rights has traditionally been viewed in the context of the collective rights of a group of people, not simply the personal rights of an individual. To a great extent, this approach is locked in China's own traditions. Being historically the country with the longest tradition of an agricultural economy, China has grown and developed from the villages and social conventions have emphasised the collective interest of the village over the personal interests of any individual. Agricultural efficiency in China has always been linked to collective management of individual plots. This cooperation by different families at the village level has, over 4000 years of farming, always proved to be the most effective means of promoting the village's own prosperity. Where one family tries to act too independently or fails to cooperate, the interests of the village would suffer as a whole. To a great extent, many of the dictums preached by Confucius largely amounted to a crystallisation or philosophical interpretation of this existing social order.

In times of harvest, the collaboration of all village families in harvesting the plots consecutively always proved to be more effective in getting all the crops in before the cold season or pests set in, than if each individual family acted in isolation. In times of famine, the villages where food was distributed and shared equally between families were the ones that survived intact. Therefore, in China, the very survival of the village economy has necessitated upholding collective rights and not allowing any one person to exercise their own individual rights at the expense of the group.

One meaning of the word 'humanism' is concern with the interests of the human race, not the individual. The Chinese concept fundamentally differs from the Western concept of human rights. In the West, particularly in America, the rights of the individual are promoted in isolation from those of the group; the often negative impact on the group which can result is rarely given consideration. Take, for example, the issue of firearms control. In America, the right to own and carry a firearm is enshrined in the US Constitution.

This right was probably rooted in economic necessity 200 years ago when the Constitution was adopted, a time when America was a frontier society and firearms were the only protection white settlers had against wild animals and other very real threats. Two hundred years later, however, the right to bear arms has been taken to extremes. A plethora of weapons circulates throughout America, threatening the life of anyone who walks the streets after sundown—unless armed themselves. This is a scenario which could not be imagined in China, a scenario where individual rights have taken precedence over the welfare of the wider community.

In China, people are not allowed to own or carry their own firearms unless they are in the military, the police, or serving in an authorised security capacity. No individual in Chinese society has any right of access to any firearm as part of his individual human rights. This, however, in the minds of most Chinese, is a fair trade-off, as they are comparatively free to walk the streets of any urban area at any time of the night without fear. China's public parks are regularly filled with people during the pre-dawn hours, exercising or practising t'ai chi without any fear of being mugged or assaulted, an impossible scenario in any urban park in America, where even the elderly are in danger of being raped and murdered.

CONCEPTS OF HUMAN RIGHTS

The basic concept of collective human rights in China is rooted in a simple economic objective: in a society of 1.3 billion people living in a land with finite agricultural resources, feeding the people must come first. The key concern of each individual living in China today is to simply improve his livelihood one way or another. There is no question that at this stage in China's economic development, an improvement in one's livelihood and that of one's family is the overriding consideration of every Chinese.

From the Chinese Government's own perspective in managing China's economy, individual human rights and the growth and improvement of these rights can be fostered and developed. The development of the Western concept of individual human rights, however, cannot, as a practical matter, occur at a rate or within a context which could jeopardise the greater right of society to improve its livelihood. The mandate of the Government is to improve the livelihood of Chinese society as a whole. The Chinese Government's concept of human rights might sit oddly with Western institutional or government observers, viewing the situation from the isolation of their offices. However, if one wished to observe the monumental task that the Chinese Government has in attaining basic human rights, one has only to leave the air-conditioned realm of one's five-star hotel and take a train ride into the depths of China's countryside. By so doing, one can more easily grasp the enormous challenge of the Chinese Government's mandate.

Three basic principles

Three basic human rights principles or concepts are recognised in China: basic human rights (*jiben renquan*), collective human rights (*jiti renquan*), and modern human rights (*xiandai renquan*).

The concept of basic human rights encompasses individual rights, which include one's right to freedom of belief in religion and philosophy, and freedom from invasion of privacy (rights to and in one's own home, possessions and communications); political rights, which include the right to vote and participate in political activities, freedom of speech and writing, and freedom to criticise government administrative organs; and social, economic and cultural rights which include workers' and labour rights, the right to rest, the right to education, and the right to material possessions and social protection (eg, insurance and health care). In summary, when it comes to basic human rights, while China recognises the concept of individual rights, it takes the view that these rights alone do not provide protection for society as a whole. Consequently, individual rights cannot be segregated from political rights, and of equal importance are social, economic and cultural rights which are integral to the entire package of basic human rights granted under China's current social and political system.

The concept of collective human rights encompasses the right of the Chinese nation to decide its own directions and to make independent decisions in the economic, political, cultural and religious spheres, without having the process of such decision-making subjected to interference from developed imperialist nations; freedom from being subjected to colonisation by these nations; the right of the Chinese nation to independent rights and sovereignty; the right of the Chinese nation to its own economic and cultural rights and the preservation of its cultures and traditions; the right, as an under-developed country, to freely develop the economy; and the right to peaceful coexistence in the world. It is from this concept of collective human rights that China has developed the concept of modern human rights. This latter concept may at first be more difficult for Westerners to grasp if the entire human rights question is viewed through the framework of purely individual rights. To understand China's new concept of modern human rights, one must refer back to its roots—collective human rights.

Modern human rights.

Under the concept of modern human rights, human rights cannot simply be restricted to individual rights or political rights, but must simultaneously encompass the people's collective rights. From an economic point of view, the Government, in carrying out its mandate of economic development, cannot allow individuals' rights to take precedence over the combined rights of the people.

In an underdeveloped country, it is the collective right of the people to resist any outside interference or exploitation of their nation which might prevent them from developing their own national economy to improve the conditions of their livelihood. In the minds of the Chinese people today, it is the concept of modern human rights which, from a world perspective, represents the most advanced approach to the human rights question.

'Rights' provided by the State

Western concepts of human rights are based on the principle that people are born with a natural right—that of individual human beings. This is a carry-over of certain Christian principles developed in the West in a historical context completely alien to China's; in China, human rights are not a gift from Heaven but rather a condition for which the people must fight and often suffer.

This is a view which the Chinese people themselves have, from their own experiences of living in China. Western concepts of human rights often fall on uninterested ears. This could be because many of the human rights which the Chinese people expect and consider a right are not automatically provided for by Western governments, but must be bought at a price by the people. Such rights include fully subsidised medical treatment, health care, hospitalisation, food, education, housing and adequate rest. For instance, any individual, regardless of his work position, income or background, and working in a State-owned enterprise or government organisation, is entitled to automatic medical treatment at any time, whether he has the common cold or cancer. Such treatment is fully subsidised by the State through the work unit. The individual is not expected to pay anything for such treatment, or at most a very nominal amount. The provision of such care to each individual is considered a basic human right in Chinese society and one to which every individual feels automatically entitled. In this regard, while Western companies in China offer salaries at anywhere from double to 10 times the local wage levels, many Chinese will still prefer to remain with State units in order to obtain the long-term benefits provided by the State.

Housing in China is provided on an allocation basis by State units. Every family attached to a State unit is entitled to an apartment; this entitlement comes with the job. The housing situation in China is now generally far better in respect of basic standards than in Hong Kong, where housing is scarce and to some extent a traumatic problem facing each family. A family in Hong Kong will have to spend its life's savings to purchase a small unit, the standards of which are often no better than what is offered by State units across the border. It is an issue of great human rights concern in China as to how this situation may be addressed after 1997.

The benefits provided by the State explain the logic behind many Chinese preferring to work for State units rather than 'jumping into the sea' (*xia hai*) of commerce in China's transitional market situation. It surprises the Chinese that in the West, such benefits are not considered rights at all. In most of the West, there is no automatic right attached to any of these material or social conditions; rather, they are viewed as privileges to be enjoyed only by that segment of society that can afford them.

HUMAN RIGHTS AND INTERNATIONAL RELATIONS

China's sensitivity over the human rights question has, to a large extent, been misconstrued. China is not against international forums or dialogues between nations on how to improve standards of living and individual or collective rights in this regard. China is, however, adamantly against developed nations like the United States bringing the human rights issue into discussions on trade and, in turn, using it as a rallying point for developed nations to try and influence China's economic development.

Many Chinese people feel that the United States is being hypo-critical by linking the human rights issue with America's own trade deficit. First of all, they argue, the two issues should not be related. Secondly, they ask what right does the United States have to use its own standard of individual human rights, developed in the context of its own comparatively brief history, to judge other countries? What right does it have to dictate standards to other countries? Chinese often ask whether the United States Government, with its record of supporting dictatorial right-wing governments, its CIA legacy and racial minority problems, is in a position to preach to China. Chinese point out that the United States fails to recognise some of the basic human rights concepts accepted in China (women's rights, racial equality, government support for the poor) or in the larger interna-tional context of human rights between nations (the right of under-developed countries to develop economically without political, military or economic sanctions, or interference from developed countries).

From the political point of view, the United States uses its own con-cept of human rights to draw attention to the United States' argu-ments for 'punishing' China with trade sanctions.

From an economic point of view, there is great opposition in China to the United States using these arguments as an excuse to iso-late China in the community of nations and to prevent it becoming a signatory to international conventions and trade conventions (eg, GATT/WTO) which would bring China into the international com-munity, a situation which most Chinese see as consistent with trying to raise the overall standard of living. China views membership of the international community as critical to achieving the economic stan-dards which its people view as part of their collective human rights. This approach by the United States, from China's perspective, vio-lates the collective political rights of the Chinese people and their modern human rights as well.

The human rights issue is America's biggest tool for negotiations with China: human rights grasps the emotionalism and idealism that exists in America and Europe. This banner is a commonly used negotiating chip in trade relations with China.

THE WORLD CONFERENCE ON WOMEN

The World Conference on Women held in Beijing in 1995 brought with it a few questions for the West. Delegates went to China ready to make the point that Western women had been liberated and that they had something to teach their communist sisters in China. It was a big surprise for more than a few to realise that China is the equal of Western nations on this issue—this is even more remarkable considering that China's feudal traditions (eg, foot binding and concubinage) continued into the first half of this century.

While Western women may be more liberated in the sense of sexual equality, and the degree of free sex that is acceptable in Western society is still somewhat discouraged in China, no-one at the Conference was in a position to criticise the advances made by women in Chinese society, in both the business and political spheres.

The equality of women

Currently, some 46% of China's workforce is comprised of women. Women hold executive positions in many corporations in China, both private and State-owned. Women in China hold senior government positions, a fact which Chinese take pride in. For instance, in less than a decade, two women, first Chen Muhua and most recently Wu Yi, have held the position of Minister of Foreign Trade and Economic Cooperation, one of China's most powerful ministries under the State Council. There were 626 women deputies in the Eighth National People's Congress, China's parliament.

In short, Article 48 of the first Constitution of the People's Republic of China gave women equality. The Equal Rights Amendment, granting women equality with men under the American Constitution, has never been passed by Congress.

In most Chinese households, both men and women work. Both in turn are responsible for taking care of the children, picking them up from school and dropping them off. Other activities are shared, such as cooking. I have never met a Chinese male who was not capable of cooking—and who was not totally unabashed by the fact he cooked for his family. Often the grandparents live with the parents, or close by, as is the tradition in Chinese society. This is beneficial, as they are

available to take care of the children, and this in turn gives some purpose to their own lives. It also leads to a better family-oriented environment for bringing up children, thereby avoiding some of the
social problems seen in the West.

The one-child policy

The American delegates went to the Women's Conference prepared
to point out that among the peasant population of rural China there
are instances where girls are sold or given away in preference to male
children. They were eager to criticise China's one-child policy as
being the cause of this 'human rights abuse'; others criticised the
easy availability of abortion services in China as being another
example of the evil of this policy.

China has a population of 1.3 billion, 25% of the world's population in a land the size of the US; more than half of China's land mass
is either desert or uninhabitable mountains. The coastal regions, the
Yellow and Yangtze river basins, and the subtropical provinces of
Guangdong, Guangxi and Yunnan are the key rice and foodstuff-
producing areas of the country.

The one-child policy is virtually the only way China can currently
control its population: it has been implemented against a background of tradition which calls for large extended families, and a
traditional peasant outlook in the rural areas which considers the
more bodies under the household roof, the more 'mu' of fields
that can be ploughed and tended. The fact that this policy is being
implemented successfully in order to avert what could become a
food–population crisis of unimaginable proportions in the twenty-
first century if not controlled through administrative methods
in the twentieth, demonstrates the power of a guided market
economy.

While the West has been slow to criticise India or a number of
African and Latin American countries which are also having trouble
coping with accelerated population growth and suffering the death
tolls brought about by uncontrollable diseases and mass starvation, it
is quick to label China's one-child policy as a 'human rights violation'. In fact, this policy is being implemented for the very purpose
of ensuring basic human rights in China.

China's one-child policy has been implemented through widespread
sex education programs in the countryside as well as in urban areas.

Every State organisation is able to freely distribute contraceptives and couples are taught the methods of birth control as a prerequisite to obtaining a marriage licence. Such education programs, if implemented on this scale by other countries, would vastly improve population control, and in turn human living standards—not to mention the fundamentals of what human rights are all about. Such programs would be hard to introduce in the US as they would come under a barrage of protests from right-wing, anti-birth control groups.

The adventures of Harry Wu

In the run-up to the World Conference on Women in Beijing, the hottest topic of conversation in China–US circles was whether or not President Clinton's wife Hillary would attend. The only thing that might have prevented her was the fact that a freshly baptised American citizen, Harry Wu Hongda, was being held on espionage charges in China.

This case is discussed in detail here because it provides in itself a microcosm of the dynamics surrounding ongoing US–China relations in the shadow of the 'human rights' issue. It seemed amazing to many that the salvaging of China–US relations depended on China freeing Harry Wu. Congressmen, and other spokesmen from various groups in America, monopolised the screens of CNN for weeks before his release, citing China's human rights record as the reason why Hillary Clinton could not attend what was clearly to be a watershed international conference in Beijing.

The connection between the detention of Harry Wu and human rights seemed tenuous at best. Harry Wu entered China from the West, without crossing at a designated border or customs clearance point. In America, under US law, this same action, if performed on, say, the Mexican border, would be tantamount to making Harry Wu an illegal immigrant. The question is: what right does America have to tell other nations that illegal immigrants should be legal in their countries, when immigration laws are strictly enforced in the US?

The excitement over Harry Wu seemed to be linked to his so-called mission to expose prison labour in China's reform camps. This gave Wu, in the eyes of Americans, a sort of hero status, which seemed to justify the fact that Harry slipped over China's borders illegally.

Harry Wu's intention was to film the prisoners working in the reform camps. It was his intention to somehow evade a very efficient security apparatus, enter the camps, take photographs, and leave— somehow undetected. This is the sort of thing which features in action movies. The fact that, prior to his arrest, Harry Wu posed for photographers in his hotel in China, dressed like Indiana Jones, the lead character in the popular movie, 'Raiders of the Lost Ark' (complete with explorer's cowboy-style hat and neckerchief) might lead one to think that Harry just wanted to get himself arrested in a timely manner whereby he could attract a lot of publicity and still get out through diplomatic channels. In fact, this is exactly what happened.

However, the question remains: did Harry Wu do anything illegal? If an American who had forfeited his citizenship for refuge in, say, Russia, returned to America under separate guise, loaded with film gear, and wanted to photograph prisoners on death row in America, or scenes of male prisoners being raped by other male prisoners, does anyone imagine that the prison authorities, state police, or FBI would allow this ex-American anywhere near any prison? Furthermore, it is inconceivable that they would allow such an individual to take photographs randomly of such scenes and leave the country to fly back to Russia and disseminate them as anti-American propaganda. Is it any surprise that Chinese ask why America thinks it can have a double standard for judging such activities in other people's countries? Of course, some argue that reform camps exist in China, and that prisoners are forced into heavy labour; many Chinese countered at the time that chain gangs were *reintroduced* into Mississippi in 1995.

Harry Wu was tried on the basis that he had clearly been caught in the act of breaking certain laws in force in a country he had illegally entered; he was convicted and sentenced to 15 years in prison. (As a matter of interest, up until the lifting of the 'Trading with the Enemy' Act in the context of Vietnam in 1994, Americans caught doing business there were liable to at least 10 years in an American prison.)

When the Chinese court duly convicted and sentenced Harry Wu, the message was clear: China has its own laws and legal system and those breaking it will be tried accordingly, and sentenced if appropriate. Then, to the surprise of everyone, Harry Wu was escorted from the courthouse, not to prison, but to Beijing Capital Airport, where he was put aboard a plane and whisked back to the US. The second message was also clear: China could be capable of great flexibility and, where necessary, deference for American sensitivities. Hillary Clinton had little choice but to attend the Women's Conference.

The denouement to the Harry Wu case was China's diplomatic finesse. The ultimate tragedy of American diplomacy is that this was virtually lost on America's foreign policy-makers, and on the public as well. Much of the international community, however, observed the sequence of events as symbolic of China's new-style diplomacy.

PART II

REFORMS

水 落 石 出 。

When the tide goes out,
everyone can see the rocks.

—old Chinese saying

CHAPTER 4

MACRO-CONTROLS

大 畜

Daxù • Great Saving

龍 潛 大 壑 之 課 。
積 小 成 大 之 象 。

The image is of a dragon hidden in a solitary glen.
The symbol is that accumulation of small particles results in a mountain.

—I CHING

易 經

One of the teachings of Mao Zedong was the importance of self-reliance. It was his vision that China should not fall into the same trap as other developing countries, and come to rely on the political–military umbrella of a larger power, or on economic links. Mao was constantly vigilant in his determination that China would not become the dependent client of a patron state. 'Dependency', as an economic relationship, already existed between a number of ex-colonies and the nations which had colonised them, or between larger developed nations and their smaller underdeveloped neighbours—as in the case of the US and Latin America. Situations evolve where underdeveloped countries are trapped into producing agricultural goods, raw materials and energy resources to fuel the continued growth of their 'patron' states in the industrialised West. These underdeveloped or developing countries in turn become dependent upon Western commercial commodities; they become 'dependent' markets for the goods of the industrialised West with little chance of breaking out of the relationship. Mao was determined not to allow China to fall into such 'neo-colonial' relationships.

To some extent, this concern explains China's continuing policy of, on the one hand, encouraging Western investment, while, on the other, monitoring and prohibiting dominance over key domestic industrial sectors which would lead to ultimate dependency upon foreign goods and services. In opening its market, this is exactly what the PRC government wishes to avoid; it cannot totally liberate certain sectors of its economy until these sectors are strong enough to compete on an equal basis with the industrialised West.

From a Western perspective, such fears may be seen as xenophobic but, from the perspective of history, such concerns, are well grounded. For example, American policy towards Asia has always carried with it a certain undercurrent of 'Americanisation', where the local people adopt American values, to some degree. Americanisation occurred after World War II in Japan, the Philippines, Taiwan and Vietnam. The view was, if Western values could take root, a taste of so-called 'freedom', then American-style democracy could develop, creating a bulwark against the spread of communism. From a purely commercial point of view, however, it was perceived that baseball, basketball, Coke, McDonald's and other symbols of American culture would affect local values to an extent where they guaranteed markets for American products.

To a great extent, China's continued policies of encouraging foreign investment generally, while restricting and prohibiting investments in particular fields, are rooted in the principle of non-dependency upon foreign goods, services and, ultimately, in some respects, investment. China suffered throughout the 1950s, 1960s and early 1970s, largely due to its own economic and political isolation. Such isolation was caused by a combination of factors, which included a US-led Western trade embargo against China, and China's own desire to remain self-sufficient in economic growth, key production sectors and technological development.

Many of the industrialised countries of Asia (such as Japan, Singapore, Korea and Thailand) have successfully implemented a two-stage economic growth policy of import substitution followed by export promotion. Simply put, at the import substitution stage, a country will overvalue its currency in order to lower the cost of imports needed to develop its infrastructure, telecommunications and technology base. When these have been developed, the second—export promotion—stage begins, at which time the currency is devalued in order to make the country's exports competitive on the international market.

China has adopted this model. The 1980s clearly marked China's period of import substitution, when investment incentives encouraged the transfer of industrial expertise and technology while an artificially overvalued currency made consumer imports an unnecessary luxury. In the 1990s, China has embarked on the export promotion stage of growth. Successive currency devaluations have made Chinese goods competitive internationally. The recent dropping of import barriers in 1996 was aimed at gaining access to the international trade conventions and thereby boosting China's exports.

FOREIGN DEBT

Becoming financially self-sufficient as a nation was one of the key goals of the Chinese Government after 1949. This goal had tremendous psychological importance for both the Government and the people: it meant that China could achieve freedom from foreign influence and regain self-esteem lost during the colonial period before World War II and again during the Japanese occupation.

In the 1960s, China cleared the bulk of its foreign debts, most of which were Soviet. The Chinese people were proud and the Government relieved. China has since maintained a low debt burden, at levels almost unmatched when compared to other nations. To a great extent, this has been the result of a tight monetary policy which combines guided growth under the auspices of State planning with the gradual transition to market economics. Due partly to its long years of economic isolation, during which foreign commodities, services and imports generally were kept to a bare minimum, China was able to build up a reasonable level of foreign exchange reserves. In 1980, the country had a bare US$2.26 billion in reserves.

During the early years of the open door policy, China monitored its foreign exchange reserves carefully, so that by 1984 they had increased to US$14.42 billion—enough to pay for seven months of imports. The safe International Monetary Fund standard is considered to be three months. This in itself could be considered a substantial achievement for China: it put itself well into the 'safe' country category within only four years of adopting the open door policy. In 1995, only 15 years after adopting the open door policy, China had foreign exchange reserves in excess of US$69.8 billion, growing to over US$90 billion by 1996. This extraordinary growth, unmatched by any country other than Japan in recent history, was largely the result of very careful centralised monetary management.

The success of China's early initiatives in opening its economy while maintaining continued economic independence, and not falling into the debt-service dependency relationship which has been the fate of other developing countries, could, to a great extent, be seen as representing the formative stage of China's merging and blending of market reforms with strict monetary management.

Relaxation of controls

In late 1984 and early 1985, monetary controls were relaxed throughout the country. In response, billions of dollars were drained off as both enterprises and individuals embarked on a massive consumer goods spending spree which caused the Government to lose control over imports. It could be said that this was China's first encounter with popular consumerism since Liberation. While the State was experimenting with how much power it could delegate to regional governments, at this stage of economic transition, the regions were experimenting with how much they could get away with under the nose of the State.

In political terms, China was at the time undergoing a transition from personal, power-backed rule, which had prevailed at both the regional as well as Central Government levels from the 1950s to the 1970s, to a growing rule of law. In the late 1980s, this transition was far from complete, and the development of institutional financial structures remained green. Power elites in some provinces seized at the opportunities that arose through the relaxation of earlier monolithic State controls and the new freedoms offered by decentralisation, treating local bank branches as if they were their own personal treasuries and ordering financing for local projects contrary to the wishes of the Central Government. The old folk saying, 'The sky is high and the Emperor far away' was popularly quoted during this period of decentralisation.

Acting on a new policy of commercial liberalisation and granting of greater local autonomy to the regions by the Central Government, between 1 January 1984 and March 1985, China's southern island of Hainan imported 9000 vehicles, 2.86 million television sets, 250,000 videotape recorders and 322,000 motorcycles. Some commodities, which were subject to heavy duties and limited quotas in other regions, were resold to enterprises throughout China. Because of Hainan's underdevelopment, the Central Government had set an ambitious target for it: to have an economy equal to that of Taiwan within 20 years. In response to the new official policy to 'make Hainan Island get rich as soon as possible', Hainan officials felt that speculation in motor vehicles would be the best way to go.

Between 1984–85, the Government watched its carefully accumulated foreign exchange reserves drop as a host of similar import schemes flourished in China's free economic zones. As a result, China's trade deficit shot up to US$15 billion in 1985, while foreign exchange reserves plummeted from US$14.42 billion in 1984 to US$11.19 billion by March 1986. For the first time, the country had to borrow from abroad to finance its visible trade deficit, which averaged US$1–1.5 billion a month. China's foreign debt grew from US$14 billion in 1984 to US$30.2 billion in 1987.

During these years, one of China's critical problems was the management of foreign exchange at the provincial or local level. A unified system of control and supervision was not yet mature; the powers of the State Administration of Exchange Control (SAEC) were not fully developed and widely extended until 1986. During this transitional period, funds were often obtained at the local level on the basis of political power rather than actual calculated profitability. Such funds were, in fact, frequently used to import consumer goods rather than finance the development projects for which they had been earmarked under State plans.

Measures to achieve stability

In 1986, in order to take control over this situation, a number of urgent measures were adopted. The first move was to ban consumer imports and to curtail other imports. In parallel, the 'anti-bourgeoisie liberalisation' political campaign was launched which, to a large extent, used political pretexts to rail against the popular use of 'unnecessary foreign imports'. Combining 'political movements' with firm macro-economic controls indicates the transitional stage in which China found itself. The fact was that Chinese society was emerging from the shadows of the Cultural Revolution into the international trade community.

During the Cultural Revolution, political rallies were used to spark economic incentives or place parameters on popular behaviour. What the 1980s witnessed was a sort of merger between political policy directives and macro-monetary management, characterised by political campaigns and a wavering between market economics and State planning. In their efforts to reduce dependency on foreign consumer products, China's policy-makers labelled consumer frivolity 'spiritual pollution' in the 1983 campaign and 'bourgeoisie liberalisation' in 1986.

The perception of the international community, as translated by the foreign press, was that 'the Chinese government doesn't have a clear direction', or 'they take one step forwards and two back'. Those rather superficial observations led political analysts in Western think-tank institutions and academics to postulate that China's reforms were becoming a battleground between two factions, a liberal (right wing) faction headed by Deng Xiaoping that wanted capitalism, and a conservative (left wing) faction headed by Chen Yun that wanted a more leftist brand of communism. This oversimplification of China's economic reforms dominated Western headlines for over a decade. While the press may be excused, the appalling fact was that minds that should have known better allowed this interpretation to be a guiding force in foreign policy towards China.

However, in the mid-1980s, China's reforms were actually progressing, though, in the words of Deng Xiaoping, 'In crossing the river we must step slowly and be sure not to slip on the rocks'. While Deng represented one school of thought, advocating a more aggressive reform system, Chen Yun represented a more cautious approach in moving away from State planning. The thoughts of both men, however, were intertwined; in some ways, they were like different faces of the same coin. Deng's reforms took the approach of, 'Go ahead and "open the window wide and let the breeze in; if a few flies come in—then swat them!"' This differed only in focus from Chen Yun's approach—that the economy was like a bird that could 'fly free so long as it is kept inside a cage, lest it fly away'.

Each correction of the Chinese economy over the 15-year period between 1980 and 1995 represented a merger of political campaigns with macro-economic adjustments. This resulted in a gradual reduction in the political campaign element and an increase in the adaptation of more classic forms of monetary intervention. The effect of the 'anti-bourgeoisie liberalisation' propaganda and the tight foreign exchange credit and export controls was to bring the growth of total imports down from 55% in 1985 to almost zero in 1986–87. Political campaigns, however, were far less effective than the interventionist tools being adopted by the planners in Beijing. Exports during this period were aggressively promoted through incentive schemes, while 1986 saw a 15% devaluation of the Renminbi, the largest devaluation ever. This had the immediate effect of making Chinese goods cheaper, and therefore more competitive, on the international markets. At the same time, as a counter balance to an inflationary reaction to the devaluation, procedures for obtaining foreign loan approvals became more complicated. There were tighter restrictions on the issuance of foreign exchange guarantees to cover such loans. The monetary policy decisions taken in 1986, including the devaluation of the Renminbi and export incentives, helped China's current account to improve in 1987: foreign exchange reserves rose to US$15.23 billion. Much of this improvement can be credited to a sharp rise in exports, which rose by a record 30%.

The powers of the SAEC were also increased in 1986; assuming tight central control over foreign exchange, it began to monitor China's loan commitments by supervising the borrowing limits of domestic organisations. The SAEC received a new brief as an independent bureau under the State Council, reporting upwards to the State Council through the People's Bank of China (PBOC). The PBOC in turn began to take on the role of a real central bank, becoming a think-tank for monetary policy and a supervisory organ establishing credit policy parameters, and monitoring and restricting the lending activities of the commercial banks.

THE BATTLE WITH INFLATION

In 1987, a growth in trade was accompanied by an expansion of China's foreign exchange reserves, which grew from US$10.51 billion in 1986 to US$15.23 billion, estimated to be enough to cover five to six months of imports. Although 1988 proved to be China's best trading year yet, major macro-economic problems remained.

Further attempts at decentralisation, combined with an expansion of money supply, led to excessive growth in most sectors and unprecedented inflation, the country's worst since 1949. Many elderly leaders in the Central Government recalled the hyperinflation of the late 1940s when citizens pushed wheelbarrows of cash to the markets just to buy vegetables—a factor which contributed to the downfall of the corrupt Kuomintang government.

China's post-1949 experiences with inflation have always been associated with excessive cash issues. This time, it was estimated that 30–40% of China's money supply consisted of cash circulating among the populace. With so much money circulating outside the banking system, the Central Government was forced once again to print more money to alleviate the growing credit squeeze in the country, thereby further fuelling inflation. The Chinese people by this time had learnt to respond to inflation by withdrawing their money from the State-owned banks and using it to buy either goods or foreign currency on the black market. When inflation surged in mid-1988, goods which had sat on store shelves for years were soon bought up. The Renminbi rates for US and Hong Kong dollars on the black market were twice the official rates.

In the latter half of 1988, the Government responded to inflation with a sudden recentralisation, resulting in a tighter squeeze on credit and foreign exchange. Loans were withdrawn, and many infrastructural investment projects were cut at short notice. By the end of the year, the economy was headed for a slowdown, and foreign investment began to slacken off.

Premier Zhao Ziyang had realised that the drastic measure taken to accelerate growth, including the removal of State subsidies, would result in inflation. However, Zhao adopted the approach that, in order to put the Chinese economy on the right growth track for future generations, 'The current generation would need to suffer for the benefit of the future generations', at least for a while. What Zhao failed to take into account was how much the current generation would tolerate in a climate of rising prices and wage stagnation. The rise of Li Peng (viewed as an entrenched technocrat and therefore associated—largely due to his own close association with Chen Yun—with 'conservative' economic policies), was contrasted with Zhao (whose experiments with economic policy in Sichuan in the early 1980s were viewed as 'liberal'). When Zhao was raised to the position of Party Secretary at the 1987 Thirteenth Party Congress, his hands were ostensibly taken off the economic levers—at least on a day-to-day basis. This was viewed (locally as well as overseas) as a 'reversal' of the reforms against a backdrop of runaway inflation.

Inflation was probably the overwhelming factor which drove workers to join the student protests in Tiananmen Square in 1989. Most of the population was less concerned with the demands of the students, which were viewed as unrealistic, than it was with the fact that fixed wages in State-owned enterprises could not keep up with inflation driven by China's first real experience of excessive growth in 1988. Enterprise reforms had not yet caught up with agricultural reforms.

THE ECONOMY AFTER JUNE 1989

China faced a liquidity squeeze in 1990, as traditional sources of capital inflow such as foreign investment, tourism and Chinese bond issues decreased in the wake of international sentiments over the events of 4 June 1989. Foreign exchange inflows and foreign investment all but stopped, and most credit facilities had to be restructured because of projects which either fell dead or could not be financed due to the World Bank and Asian Development Bank moratorium on lending.

Foreign economic sanctions and the freezing of loans by international development and monetary institutions made it increasingly difficult for China to manage its loans in 1989–90. While loans signed before 4 June 1989 did, however, provide some capital inflow over the fourth quarter of 1989 and the first quarter of 1990, these did not cover the country's external borrowings. Consequently, China had to draw on its foreign exchange reserves, which stood at US$19.1 billion in April of 1989, to the tune of US$5–6 billion. The balance of reserves (US$13–14 billion) were sufficient to cover only three months of imports, an amount considered to be just within the safe international standard.

During this particularly difficult phase, China entered into another austerity period. Centralised regulation increased, particularly in respect of the foreign trade system where import–export controls have traditionally provided a management mechanism by which the Central Government could shore up foreign exchange reserves. Once again, restrictions were implemented in respect of imports (particularly consumer goods), which central policy planners identified as an 'unnecessary' drain on the reserves. International condemnation of the events of June 1989 and the economic sanctions that followed played right into China's trade policy, by reducing the outflow of foreign exchange.

While US boardrooms, filled with the images of Tiananmen, allowed emotion to guide corporate strategy, Chinese planners got the breathing space they needed to resist the barrage of foreign imports which had drained foreign exchange reserves. China redirected its expanding domestic production by tapping into Korean and Taiwanese investment, undaunted by political events. The result was a net increase in trade and a gradual reversal of China's trade deficit. China's productivity was able to consolidate during this period, as inflation was brought back in line with existing wage levels.

The trade deficit with the United States was soon reversed, allowing China, for the first time, to enjoy a trade surplus against the United States. With the removal of international economic sanctions and the revival of lending by the World Bank and Asian Development Bank, investment steadily began returning to China. The tourist industry revived again in 1991–92 in the wake of the Asian Games held in Beijing, leading to a flood of heavy-spending tourists from Japan and Taiwan. During these years, China's foreign exchange reserves soared, reaching an unprecedented level of US$45 billion, placing China comfortably among the 10 nations holding the world's largest foreign exchange reserves. The reserves have continued steadily upwards, doubling to US$70 billion in 1995 and to US$100 billion in 1996. With the absorption of Hong Kong's US$70 billion in foreign exchange reserves in 1997, China will nearly double its total reserves, equalling Japan as a world financial power.

The Five-year Plan System

While some may regard China's five-year plan system as a legacy of archaic Soviet-style command economics, it has in fact given China a framework for developing its modernisation programs. Each five-year plan is accompanied by a 15-year target or projection of where China's economy should be, say, two five-year plans beyond the current one. This provides clear direction and sets out specific goals. The plans are formulated through a system of continuing dialogue

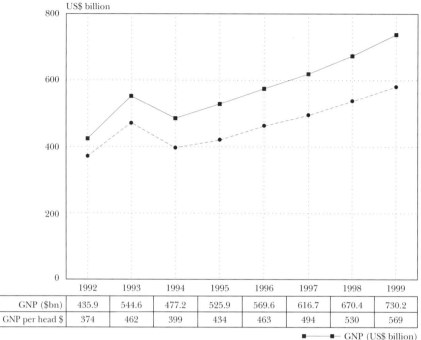

	1992	1993	1994	1995	1996	1997	1998	1999
GNP ($bn)	435.9	544.6	477.2	525.9	569.6	616.7	670.4	730.2
GNP per head $	374	462	399	434	463	494	530	569

■——■ GNP (US$ billion)

●----● GNP per head (US$)

CHINA'S GNP 1992–99: ACTUAL AND PROJECTED

that takes place at and between various levels of government. The commissions, ministries and bureaus that operate under the State Council report back to the Council on the progress in their respective sectors. The State Council uses this information to compile the next five-year plan and then submits it to the Politburo of the Communist Party of China. The Politburo ratifies the plan and passes it on to its Standing Committee which then submits it as a proposal for consideration at the National People's Congress. Each plan is discussed at Politburo and National People's Congress meetings held in Beijing and, when adopted, its details are disseminated back down the line to the commissions, ministries and bureaus under the State Council.

China's development during the 1980s was characterised by the 'Four Modernisations', a program of cautious liberalisation of the economy combined with opening up to foreign investment and trade—often on an experimental basis concentrated in designated coastal areas. China's target in the 1980s was to achieve 'a level of basic standards' (*wen bao*). The second stage of China's development, from 1990 to 1995, was marked by the Eighth Five-Year Plan. The objective during this period was to reduce the level of poverty and raise the people's livelihood to 'a good standard' (*xiao kang*). The third stage is the current Ninth Five-Year Plan (1996–2000). China's stated goal during this period is to raise the economic standards even further, bringing China to the level of 'an affluent society' (*geng jia kuan yu*).

In the 1980s, Deng Xiaoping's stated objective was to quadruple the economy by the year 2000. To achieve this, the Chinese economy would have to attain a GNP level of 5765 billion yuan by that date. During the Politburo and the National People's Congress meetings in Beijing during March 1996, when the Ninth Five-Year Plan was adopted, it was announced that China had achieved this goal in 1995, five years ahead of schedule.

Throughout the Eighth Five-Year Plan (1990–95), China maintained a growth rate of 12% a year. During this period, inflation reached an unprecedented high of 22.5% in 1994, resulting in a nationwide clamp-down by the Central Government. A combination of tight credit control and monetary restraint brought inflation back down to 15% in 1995. Through continuing monetary intervention and macro-economic controls, inflation further reduced to 10% and now stands at 7.7%. This remarkable monetary engineering has brought about a situation where growth is higher than inflation. In 1995, GNP was up 75.9% over 1990. The population living at the poverty level dropped although, since the previous decade, the population had grown by 300 million.

The current Five-Year Plan is targeting an annual growth rate of 8% and an inflation rate of less than 8%. The medium to long-term target is to double GNP between the years 2000 and 2010. In order to achieve this, growth will need to be continually monitored while tight credit controls will have to be maintained; there will also be limited issues of new currency into the system. During this period, China will benefit from higher savings among the local population, a higher reserve rate, and systematic and guided economic growth. On the other hand, people will continue to face difficulties in respect of limited credit available for borrowing purposes, limited cash available for enterprise transformation and growth, and tight employment conditions.

Looking back on the road that China has travelled, the changes and advances are unbelievable; the lifestyle of the Chinese today would have been incomprehensible only 15 years ago. However, China's growth hasn't come without costs. China has battled with inflation and periodic drains on its foreign exchange reserves resulting from sporadic bouts of importing goods. However, through a complex and uniquely Chinese combination of control mechanisms, beginning with political campaigns and eventually evolving into the kind of sophisticated monetary intervention applied in Europe, China has achieved an impressive record of economic growth and foreign exchange reserve accumulation.

CHAPTER 5

STRUCTURES

恆

Heńg • Constancy

日 月 常 明 之 課 。
四 時 不 沒 之 象 。

The image is of the sun and moon always shining brightly.
This symbol is that the always changing seasons perpetuate the creation of things.
—I CHING

易 經

Following Liberation in 1949, the Chinese Communist Party adopted the Soviet model of government as a structural framework for the People's Republic. Nothing can be changed by debating the quirky turns of history, but it is worth reflecting for a moment on what creative combinations might have emerged if the Chinese Communist Party had been given the same opportunities as the Kuomintang regime in Taiwan—that is, US aid and technical support. In his memoirs on World War II, journalist Theodore White recalled the frustration he felt when filing his reports on the escalating popular support for the Chinese Communist Party, which was like a snowball gaining in momentum and volume as it rolls downhill. His reports were heavily censored by the managing editor of *Time* magazine, who felt obliged to report news consistent with the political views of Washington DC.

After 1949, China in fact reached out for direct relations with the US, a gesture which was deliberately ignored by the then right-wing anti-communist bloc in Washington. John Foster Dulles refused to shake Zhou Enlai's hand in Geneva in 1958. In the decades to follow, both Vietnam and Cuba would try to establish direct relations with the US, only to be rejected, leaving them no other option than to turn to the Soviet Union for support. In China's case, the break-through finally came when left-wing journalist Edgar Snow visited Mao Zedong in 1970; it was during Snow's visit that Mao invited President Nixon to China.

Throughout this period of isolation, Mao himself remained extremely wary of the Soviet Union and Soviet intentions towards China. He privately criticised their system and remained constantly frustrated with its rigidity. Commenting one day, he said, 'When I say, "Learn from the Soviet Union", we don't have to learn how to shit and piss from the Soviet Union too, do we? I'd rather not learn from the Soviet Union. I want to learn from the United States.'

Nevertheless, China adopted a system of government more or less based on that of the Soviet Union, with a State Council serving as the executive branch of government, and various commissions and min-istries below. This system was to be borrowed by the Socialist Republic of Vietnam and, in turn, the People's Democratic Republic of Laos.

A PYRAMID OF POWER

The Government of the People's Republic of China is structured like a pyramid. This pyramid can be seen as consisting of various over-lapping pyramids, each representing a different commission or min-istry, and each linked at the top through the ever-revolving sphere of State-level politics. Depending on where key political figures stand in relation to the players at the centre, one can determine the power of the ministry or commission concerned, and the relation of that body to the centre. By ascertaining its status compared to similar bodies, one can accurately judge the ultimate scope of power that body wields throughout the system as a whole. (The Appendix sets out the power structure in China.)

The National People's Congress

The National People's Congress serves as the highest law-making body in the country. It consists of representatives elected from the various provinces, special regions and autonomous zones. As the National People's Congress meets only when sessions are called, on an annual or biannual basis, a special Standing Committee of the National People's Congress carries on the coordinating duties and functions related to the drafting and vetting of laws and regulations at the national level.

Contrary to Western perceptions, the electoral process for the National People's Congress is very democratic in nature. Electoral procedures are also structured like a pyramid, working from the grassroots upwards. Candidates are first selected at the lower county level for participation in the people's committees at that level. These committees in turn select representatives to attend meetings at the larger district level; the district people's committees select representatives to attend the municipal people's congresses, which in turn select representatives to attend the provincial or autonomous zone people's congresses—from these congresses are chosen the people who will attend the National People's Congress held in Beijing. While not a direct voting procedure, this is democratic system.

The State Council

The State Council established under the National People's Congress serves as the executive branch of state. Whereas the United States has a president serving in the executive function backed by a virtually powerless vice president and secretaries of different departments (eg, Secretary of State, of Defence, of the Interior) appointed by the president himself, the State Council today has one premier, six vice premiers, and eight state councillors. In this regard, the State Council is an executive body with a collective as opposed to individualistic decision-making structure; it can, in fact, present more diversified views than the US president's cabinet.

The State Council is very much a collective governing council. It consists of the Premier who, for all intents and purposes, serves as the highest authority of State. (The positions of Chairman and Vice Chairman of State in China are now largely ceremonial.) Under the Premier are a number of Vice Premiers, each of whom has a brief for coordinating a different set of sectors, whether these be economic, industrial, financial, social or cultural. Under each Vice Premier are a number of State Councillors who are each in turn responsible for a number of specific sectors and the ultimate coordination of guiding policies for these sectors.

To move into a position of State Councillor or Vice Premier requires an enormous commitment of time in order to understand the economic conditions, structures and problems of China. For most of these leaders, this is a life-long commitment requiring knowledge and experience far beyond that attained by any president or vice president in America (at least over the past three decades). The experience and technical knowledge required to move into a position of leadership in China today can be contrasted with some other systems, where all one needs to be elected are substantial financial backing and a good advertising campaign.

Most of these leaders live simple lives, although the State provides for their everyday needs. The home of Li Peng, for instance, is a simple concrete block-style house, in a very inconspicuous street in Beijing. Vice Chairman Rong Yiren lives in a courtyard compound in relative simplicity in a lane tucked away behind ordinary houses. This atmosphere of frugality and understatement contrasts sharply with the lifestyles which many Western politicians enjoy at the expense of their taxpayers.

Commissions and ministries

Under the State Council, there are the State-level commissions; these serve a purpose similar to that of a ministry, but have a higher ranking. For instance, there is the State Planning Commission, the State Commission on Education, the State Commission for Science and Technology and the State Commission for Ethnic Minorities.

On the next level are the ministries which, though at a level lower then the State-level commissions, serve a similar function and report directly to the State Council. Each ministry is responsible for overseeing specific functions and supervising the administrative aspects of its particular sector of the economy. There are two main kinds of ministry, the 'comprehensive ministries', which supervise general matters on a cross-sectoral basis (the Ministry of Trade, the Ministry of Transport and Communications and the Ministry of Finance are examples), and 'sectoral' or 'industrial ministries' which supervise specific industries or sectors of the economy (the Ministry of Light Industry, the Ministry of Textiles and the Ministry of Coal are examples of this type of ministry).

THE TRANSITION TO MARKET ECONOMICS

From the 1950s to the early 1980s, the State virtually dominated the entire enterprise sector. Each enterprise reported directly to the ministry under whose administration it fell, and could not enter into commercial contracts independently. When foreign investors first started entering into contracts with Chinese enterprises in the 1980s, whether these were simply trade contracts or investment contracts, the administrative ministry concerned had to be party to the contract. For instance, if a foreign company wished to enter into a contract to buy toys from a toy-manufacturing enterprise in Shanghai, the local Light Industry Bureau under the National Light Industry Ministry would have to be a signatory to the contract. The enterprise had no authority to enter into such a contract independently.

By the mid-1980s, changes in policy parameters allowed State-owned enterprises to enter into contracts directly with foreign companies for the purpose of export sales or the establishment of foreign investment enterprises. In parallel, the industrial ministries began to refocus. There was a reduction in the degree of direct management over the affairs of the enterprises in the industrial sector and greater concentration on administrative work, the monitoring of the industries and formulation of industrial policies.

The powerful State Planning Commission also felt an erosion of its once almost plenary authority, as more and more sectors were released from the dictates of a planned economy. The structure of command economics disintegrated as the market began to dominate year-end planning which soon took on a new and entirely commercial focus at the enterprise level.

The role of the commissions

In order to reorient the role of the industrial or sectoral ministries within the system and find a transitional medium between market economics and a planned economy, the following key reforms were implemented. Starting in the late 1980s, measures were taken to separate the administrative and regulatory government functions of industrial sector ministries from the commercial operations of enterprises: administrative functions were centralised in large think-tank macro planning/guidance commissions or ministries, while all the commercial activities were carried out by the enterprises. The market economy could flourish with little restriction or inhibition, while the State directed the macro-development of the economy. The State had the power to control the merger or restructuring of large State-owned enterprises, or encourage joint ventures with foreign investment, rather than permit widespread bankruptcy due to the market reforms. Critical to this process were the State-level commissions, which served principally to frame macro-policies.

During the 1950s and through to the early 1980s, the State Planning Commission wielded enormous power as China adopted the Soviet-style 'command economy' system, where the State specified the products to be manufactured and the volume of such products—market factors were largely irrelevant. Enterprises were so focused on meeting production targets that issues of quality control were ignored, with the result that quality of production plunged during these years.

With the adoption of market economics, the State Planning Commission's role began to adjust. Rather than simply dictating targets, and dishing out funds to be used to meet these targets, it began coordinating economic policy between different sectors, a function for which it was not prepared. Therefore, in the 1980s, Premier Zhao Ziyang established the State Commission for Reform of Economic Systems to provide overall coordination of the often polemic problems inherent in China's transitional economy. Throughout the late 1980s, this body served as both a powerful think-tank for the State Council and a pioneering force behind many of China's enterprise and financial sector reforms. These reforms, however, had the effect of creating wide disparity between agricultural and urban wage structures against a backdrop of hyperinflation caused by unexpected unprecedented growth.

Speculation and inflation

The traumatic events which occurred in 1989 have been interpreted entirely in a political light. The events of that year, and their culmination in the mass protests in Tiananmen Square, need, however, to be carefully understood in the context of China's erupting economy and the dichotomies which resulted at the time.

The initial liberalisations of the 1980s and the introduction of the 'self-responsibility system' (*chengbaozhi*) led to a loosening of controls over prices, and the implementation of services at the regional level. Raw material speculation combined with demands on what was then an inefficient transport sector sparked inflation on a scale not seen since Liberation in 1949. The immediate effect was to damage State enterprise production: State enterprises were simply unprepared for the situation and were unable to obtain raw materials to meet production targets. This in turn translated into a crisis involving workers' wages and subsidies.

Events in 1989 ran something like this. Production problems created rampant inflation and people reacted to inflation in the only way they could, by dumping currency in favour of goods. Mass buying sprees erupted throughout the country, which further drove prices to unprecedented highs. The business of speculating on raw materials became so heady that the raw materials themselves never reached the factories, as old contracts were simply ignored in favour of new offers to buy at price levels that had rocketed. Inevitably, State enterprises failed, one after another, to meet production targets because they lacked supplies. The result was that workers' wages could not keep up with inflation, driving workers to join the student protests in Tiananmen Square.

A socialist market economy

Following Zhao Ziyang's fall from political grace in the wake of the events of June 1989, the State Commission for Reform of Economic Systems remained a key think-tank organisation, reporting to Premier Li Peng. The early 1990s saw the emergence of a 'socialist market economy', as Government bodies continued to function in a traditionally political manner in administering various economic sectors, while enterprises within these sectors followed the market. The obvious theoretical conflicts inherent in a 'socialist market economy' model became irrelevant when Deng defined this new theory as having 'Chinese characteristics', thereby blessing its very eclectic nature.

It became apparent to the Central Government leadership that, in order to implement a market economy on an efficient basis, key reforms would have to be made to the administrative nature and very structured organisation of certain existing political bodies. It was felt that a single administrative body was needed to coordinate the various commissions and ministries, and to formulate unified development directives. Throughout 1990, the Central Party Standing Committee carried out an internal review of this problem. In October, Jiang Zemin addressed the Central Government, and in the course of his address, revealed two important internal Party decisions: the necessity to formally adopt a market economy model; and the necessity of establishing a single macro-management body at the Central Government level to coordinate economic policies and specific administrative functions of various commissions and ministries.

As already described, the political structure in China was pyramid-like, with each commission, ministry or bureau exerting its own powers and authority. In moving from a command to a market economy, the necessity to coordinate these various spheres of administrative power became more acute. For instance, if the Ministry of Energy needs coal in order to fuel generators at an electricity plant, it must coordinate with the Ministry of Coal to assure that coal supplies may be provided on a continuous basis. Assuming both ministries can find common ground on the supply issue, then they must in turn coordinate with the Ministry of Transportation to ensure that rail and road lines guarantee the coal can be transported on a regular basis. Needless to say, such coordination is not a simple matter when you have multiple ministries each with their own power bases and concerns over political territory, not to mention the various personalities who would definitely involve themselves and the local regional conflicts which arise when supplies must cross provincial boundaries.

In order to address this very issue, in July 1991, the State Council issued a notice to establish the Production Office of the State Council which would monitor production and coordinate services among the various industrial sectors, while simultaneously coordinating functions between different ministries. The State Council notice established the principle that China would begin to adopt an 'economic economy', not a planned economy model, while still retaining centralised administration over production and the development of key industrial sectors.

A MITI with Chinese characteristics

Shanghai Mayor Zhu Rongji was brought onto the State Council by Jiang Zemin to run the Production Office. Zhu Rongji had served successfully as the Vice Chairman of the Economic Commission (which was abolished in 1988 largely due to redundancy resulting from the overlapping functions of Zhao Ziyang's pet State Commission for Reform of Economic Systems). He was therefore the logical choice to head up the Production Office, which would have a role similar to that of the former State Economic Commission.

The role of the Production Office, however, had limitations, as China was moving away from State planning and the old production-target approach to development. Issues of distribution and retail sales were becoming more important in the view of the social transformations that were taking place. Zhu Rongji soon realised the potential power of his new organisation. Consequently, one year later, in July 1992, he proposed that the authority of the Production Office be extended to include directing development and macro-economic policy in addition to monitoring and coordinating production. His proposal was accepted, and the organisation renamed the Economy Trade Office of the State Council.

Under Zhu Rongji's guidance, the Economy Trade Office grew in importance, touching every aspect of China's growing and booming economy. In 1993, it was proposed, before a full session of the National People's Congress, that the organisation be expanded into a full-blown commission under the State Council. The proposal was accepted and the State Economy and Trade Commission came into being. In the minds of Jiang Zemin and Zhu Rongji, the State Economy and Trade Commission was to be modelled along the lines of Japan's superministry, the powerful Ministry of International Trade and Industry (MITI), providing guidance on economic policy as well as industrial policy. After establishing the State Economy and Trade Commission, however, the Central Government had to decide how to develop it into a MITI with 'Chinese characteristics'.

Three options were considered. The first option was to abolish all the industrial ministries (eg, the Ministry of Light Industry, the Ministry of Textiles, the Ministry of Coal and the Ministry of Chemical Industry) and consolidate their functions into departments of the State Economy and Trade Commission. The second option was to abolish a selection of 10 industrial ministries and consolidate them as departments under the State Economy and Trade Commission—this would be an experiment and the new system would be closely monitored. The third option was to transform two selected ministries into 'associations', acting as quasi-regulatory bodies though also assuming the role of chambers or commerce, before proceeding with further experimentation.

The Central Government chose the last of the three options, being the most conservative approach. The Ministry of Light Industry and the Ministry of Textile Industry were subsequently transformed into the Light Industry and Textile associations respectively with 1995 the target year to review the first stage of experimentation. However, this review did not take place until 1996, at which time the viability of the other options was again discussed. While Zhu Rongji pushed for the first option, a total transformation, Li Peng won out with the more conservative second approach. Ten industrial ministries are being slated as a pilot experiment.

Throughout the 1980s, MITI was a major factor in Japan's growth, coordinating both industrial and trade policies. While Japan had adopted an entirely market economy, MITI provided the parameters to guide free market growth, cutting back inefficiency and waste and, through its enormous research system and network, identifying paths of growth for Japan's industrial sector. Through the State Economy and Trade Commission, therefore, China is adopting, or at least experimenting with the adoption of, a model similar to MITI. It is now in the process of streamlining government bodies, eliminating those industrial administrative ministries which are becoming redundant as China moves further away from State planning and closer towards a system of guided market economics.

It is envisioned that, one by one, the various industrial ministries will be dismantled. The administrative and policy apparatus of these ministries will be absorbed into the State Economy and Trade Commission, where it will serve a departmental function. The remaining functions of these ministries, such as those involving market/industrial research and coordination between the enterprises under their control, will be separated into non-government associations or chambers of commerce appropriate to the industrial sector concerned. The role of the State Planning Commission will naturally reduce as China leaves the embrace of State planning generally and moves into a more market-driven economy; its coordination functions are now gradually being absorbed into the new structure evolving within the State Economy and Trade Commission. It is not unlikely that, one day, the State Planning Commission may itself become obsolete—at least, its role will become reduced.

The creation and development of the State Economy and Trade

Commission represents the new dynamics unfolding within China today. The emphasis on the softer approach of guided economics as opposed to the former heavy hand of State planning indicates a shift of focus from command to coordination. The rise of the State Economy and Trade Commission as China's MITI of the twenty-first century means that a coordinated industrial and trade policy will focus industrial development and guide production, thus making China a more efficient economy domestically and a more competitive one internationally.

CHAPTER 6

TRADE

同 人

Tóngrén • Fellowship

遊 魚 從 水 之 課 。
二 人 分 金 之 象 。

The image is a fish in water, a creature 'in its own element'.
The symbol is of money being divided between two persons.

—I CHING

易 經

The first British trade delegation to China was in the late eighteenth century and was led by a Lord Macartney. The delegation had to travel north of Beijing, beyond the Great Wall to Chengde, the imperial hunting retreat of the Qing emperors, in order to arrange a meeting with the Emperor Qian Long. The Chinese viewed the British as 'barbarians'. A meeting with the Emperor himself was not appropriate or in accordance with palace protocol. The British insisted. A meeting could be arranged but not in the Fangzheng Palace. A compromise was struck: the Emperor would receive Lord Macartney in a Mongolian yurt which was reserved for meetings with other 'barbarians' such as Mongolians and Urghurs who also came to pay homage to the Emperor from time to time.

Lord Macartney saw this audience not as an occasion to pay homage to the Emperor but as the beginning of trade relations between the two countries—on British terms, of course. This was historically the commencement of Western–Chinese misunderstandings over trade relations. The Emperor's response to Britain's King George III affronted British sensibilities.

> Swaying the wide world, I have but one aim in view, namely to maintain a perfect governance and to fulfil the duties of the State; strange and costly objects do not interest me. If I have commanded that the tribute offerings sent by you, O King, are to be accepted, this was solely in consideration for the spirit which prompted you to dispatch them from afar. Our dynasty's majestic virtue has penetrated into every country under Heaven, and Kings of all nations have offered their costly tribute by land and sea. As your Ambassador can see for himself, we possess all things. I set no value on objects strange or ingenious, and have no use for your country's manufactures. This then is my answer to your request to appoint a representative at my Court, a request contrary to our dynastic usage, which would only result in inconvenience to yourself. I have expounded my wishes in detail and have commanded your tribute Envoys to leave in peace on their homeward journey. It behooves you, O King, to respect my sentiments and to display even greater devotion and loyalty in the future, so that, by perpetual submission to our Throne, you may secure peace and prosperity for your country hereafter.

Two centuries later, in 1994, US Foreign Secretary Warren Christopher threatened China with 301 sanctions. Foreign Minister Qian Jichen's response was that Christopher would have a hard time answering to the American people, who would not be able to afford to buy shoes when Chinese-manufactured goods became prohibitively expensive due to US tariffs. When the US threatened trade sanctions worth US$2 billion again in May 1996, China's Foreign Trade Minister, Wu Yi, warned that there would be 'eye-for-eye' countersanctions, threatening to slap 100% duties on US consumer imports.

INITIAL TRADE REFORMS

China's foreign trade system grew from the Soviet system which emerged from the Lenin–Stalin era. Before the reforms introduced in 1978, the Soviet foreign trade model adopted by China was characterised by a total State monopoly and control over trade, as exercised through designated foreign trade companies. As the Soviet-style command economy prevailed, production was carried out according to the dictates of State planning. There was no creative production, as no market conditions existed.

Enterprises were not concerned whether they earned money or lost—they were concerned only with meeting production deadlines and targets. Profitability was only an issue with foreign trade companies. As State-owned enterprises never had direct contact with either their customers or the market, they had no idea about quality control, customer needs, or even the marketability of their products. From the management point of view, profits and losses were irrelevant as the enterprise was only responsible for meeting production targets. Given China's low foreign exchange reserves at the time, trade policy restricted imports, as support was only provided for exports. Customs duties during this time served no purpose, as imports were limited to only those imports required under State plans.

This was the situation from the 1950s to the 1970s. There was also a certain degree of nationalism involved in only producing and consuming Chinese rather than foreign products. To some extent, this represented an extreme reaction against the fears of 'dependency'. On the other hand, China had no alternative, given the American trade embargo against China following Liberation. This embargo carried strong political implications for America's allies in the Western world, which grew more acute from the 1960s onwards as America became increasingly engaged in war in Indo–China, on the justification that it was containing the growth of Chinese communism. Though China had little option but to follow the Soviet command economy model, this model did have credibility. The Soviet Union was the only country offering logistical support and trade credits and it was China's most viable compensation trade (goods for goods) partner, given the hard currency crunch both countries were experiencing. Unfortunately, the Soviet model was the only logical Western model available to China, given the lack of information it had on any other model due to its isolation by the Western world.

THE INTERNATIONAL TRADE EMBARGO

China's economy suffered enormously from the international embargo: it had to rely entirely on internally generated production.

In order to obtain precious foreign exchange, China could not rely on natural market conditions as such conditions did not exist due to the embargo. China therefore had to rely on creative means of raising foreign exchange income within the context of a command economy model. China's first initiative in this regard was to concentrate on the production of certain goods and commodities which it realised had an existing market overseas, such as Chinese arts and crafts, medicines and tea. These items were produced and sourced through designated trading companies which were allowed to develop direct trade links with the outside world, thereby earning foreign exchange directly for the State.

The Western press at this time colourfully presented the activities of these trading companies and events like the annual Guangzhou Trade Fair as activities reverting back to the Qing dynasty when foreign trading companies were permitted to trade only at designated points and only through authorised Mandarin officials. This perception was later reinforced when China opened the four Special Economic Zones and the 14 coastal cities. Comparisons were made between the cities selected and those which entertained foreign communities during the post-Opium War 'open door' period of another era.

The four Special Economic Zones were Shenzhen, Shekou, Zhuhai and Xiamen (Hainan came later, in 1988). They offered incentives mainly in the form of tax breaks for investors and soon became showcases of development. The 14 coastal cities were major cities which were declared 'open' to investment in 1985—although they were never really closed (that is, not open) before. Basically, the Government sought to channel investment into these industrial and population centres on the coast by offering incentives and tax breaks in order to accelerate development. Deng advocated a policy of developing the coastal regions first and then worrying about the hinterland. Others took a different line, feeling that growth should be balanced from the beginning. Deng, however, won out.

The Renminbi–US dollar rate was fixed at 1:1, mainly because China did not adopt an international gold standard, but also because China did not engage in direct currency trading and because national production demanded that the Renminbi be fixed at the same rate as the US dollar in line with the practices of a command economy. Simply put, State planning dictated a simplistic pegging of the Renminbi to the US dollar because there were no trade influences to speak of at the time.

Also at this time, China did not participate in any of the international trade conventions—as with the United Nations, where recognition was given to Taiwan but not China, the US veto made China's access to them impossible. The US veto was in line with US policy to isolate China both economically and politically. China's reaction was a policy of non-alignment. The spirit of non-alignment was growing in intensity among certain developing countries, particularly in Asia during the 1950s and 1960s. Given its forced isolation and non-participation in any conventions, China found expression for its own independent position and policy of non-dependency.

OVERHAULING THE TRADING SYSTEM

The planning factor inherent in China's earlier command economy has become less and less significant in the overall picture of China's trading activities as step-by-step market economics take over. The development of China's economy since Liberation roughly falls into

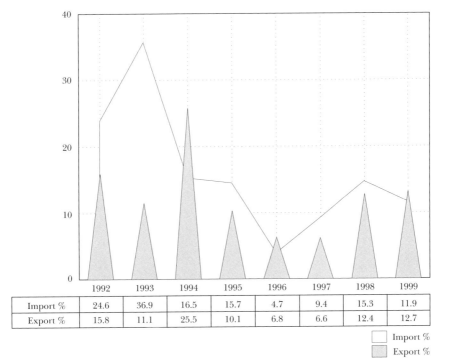

	1992	1993	1994	1995	1996	1997	1998	1999
Import %	24.6	36.9	16.5	15.7	4.7	9.4	15.3	11.9
Export %	15.8	11.1	25.5	10.1	6.8	6.6	12.4	12.7

Import %
Export %

EXPORT AND IMPORT OF GOODS: ACTUAL AND PROJECTED

four stages: 1949–79, command economy; 1980–89, planned economy; 1990–95, guided market economy; and, from 1996, a market economy with State intervention.

The reforms introduced after Deng's ascendancy at the Eleventh Party Congress in 1978 necessitated a complete overhaul of China's trading system in line with internal reforms of State-owned enterprises, the means of production, and the restrained use of the State planning apparatus as a tool for economic development.

The first of these changes involved the formerly bureaucratic foreign trade corporations, each of which was required to open its own multiple channels for foreign trade, thereby widening the previously narrow scope of trade which had been tied to the production channels. The foreign trade corporations were basically being forced to function and survive as regular trading companies finding diversified sources of domestic goods to meet international market needs. This move was accompanied by the gradual granting of export privileges to one State-owned factory after another. At the first stage, enterprises could source their own overseas buyers, provided that the foreign trade corporations served as 'agent' or third party to the contract. As the foreign trade corporations began to diversify, however, certain factories were allowed to trade directly with overseas partners.

During this time, the State provided the trading companies with subsidies in the form of a commission in Renminbi against a percentage of products exported; this measure was aimed at encouraging exports for the purpose of raising foreign exchange revenues for the State. Even if the State lost money on these subsidies, such losses fell within the context of a planned economy, and were perfectly acceptable as the intention was to raise foreign exchange for the State. Subsequent moves removed the subsidies so that trading companies had to trade on the basis of pure market economics and profitability rather than allow them to rely on State subsidies to make ends meet.

The decentralisation process continues, with a growing number of enterprises becoming capable of engaging in direct trade; the major trading corporations are responsible for their own profits and losses as opposed to implementing State plans. In parallel, the former monopolist trading companies have begun serving, not so much as government agencies implementing trade policies and earning for the State, but as independent foreign trading companies along the lines of the 'soga-soshas' of Japan.

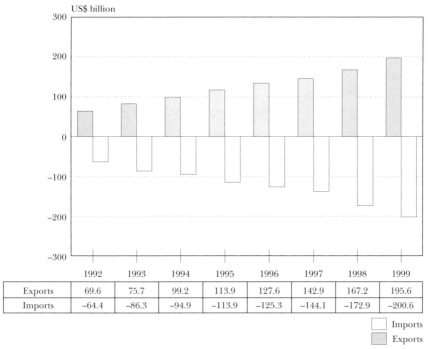

	1992	1993	1994	1995	1996	1997	1998	1999
Exports	69.6	75.7	99.2	113.9	127.6	142.9	167.2	195.6
Imports	−64.4	−86.3	−94.9	−113.9	−125.3	−144.1	−172.9	−200.6

☐ Imports
▨ Exports

MERCHANDISE EXPORTS AND IMPORTS: ACTUAL AND PROJECTED

Trading rights and tariffs

Foreign investment incentives in line with trade policy further encouraged investment involving technology transfer in the industrial sectors. The intention was to develop a domestic infrastructure base capable of producing commodities which could initially replace imports as part of an import substitution policy. These commodities would subsequently be exported, forming the basis of an export promotion policy. Since the opening of China's economy in 1978, trading rights have been granted specifically to trading corporations or designated enterprises by the Ministry of Foreign Trade and Economic Cooperation (MOFTEC). It is now China's intention to move towards a situation where, shortly, broad trading permissions will be given to enterprises in China generally. In the future, such rights will be extended to foreign investment enterprises; such foreign trade operations have already begun in a pilot scheme in Waigaoqiao Zone of Pudong Special Zone.

Customs duties used to be high on certain imported products which the State wanted to restrict, as they were deemed unnecessary commodities not related to production or technology transfer. Now customs duties are being rationalised to allow for free trading, as China moves into the export promotion phase of economic development.

Unified tariff conditions are key to gaining entry to the World Trade Organization (WTO); entry will pull China out of the perpetual bilateral trade bargaining process with the US and onto a level playing field with the world's major trading countries. This in turn will allow China to have better access to the world's markets for Chinese products. With an established infrastructure base developed through investment promotion attached to an import substitution policy in the 1980s, China has succeeded in launching into a full export promotion mode in the 1990s.

Achieving international standards

It is clearly China's intention to enter the World Trade Organization as quickly as possible. China's application for entry has already been held up for 10 years, largely due to the policy of certain Western countries to 'contain' China's economic advances, which can only be enhanced upon entry.

Economic conditions within the country permitting, China has gradually implemented a program of reforms to bring its trading system in line with international standards. Steps include rationalisation of the foreign trade corporation system and extension of trading rights, first to domestic and then to foreign enterprises (as already mentioned). The phasing out of former foreign exchange restrictions and the adoption of an interbank market system will lead to the convertibility of the Renminbi. China's own banking and financial services sector is gradually opening to foreign participation by first licensing foreign banks that are limited to foreign exchange business only, and then extending this in the near future to Renminbi transactions (first on an experimental basis extending permissions with approvals gradually but consistently over time).

The United States has consistently mixed non-trade issues with trade issues—to some extent, this is due to the fact that China's trade and related financial service sector reforms cannot be denied by the international community. Therefore, a successful blocking of China's entry to the WTO can only be achieved by moving the goalposts and erecting barriers in areas concerning standards which may

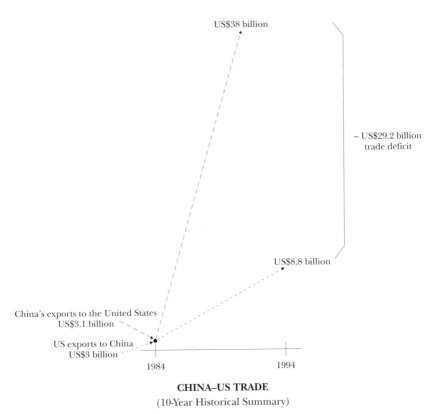

US$38 billion

– US$29.2 billion
trade deficit

US$8.8 billion

China's exports to the United States
US$3.1 billion

US exports to China
US$3 billion

1984   1994

CHINA–US TRADE
(10-Year Historical Summary)

not be attainable by China immediately—at least, according to fixed perceptions in the United States.

The first issue which always comes to mind is human rights. This issue is discussed at length in Chapter 3, and therefore will not be examined here, except to say that China does not believe that an issue as philosophical as differing standards or, better said, approaches to human rights, should be entangled with commercial trade.

The second issue involves intellectual property protection. There is no question that counterfeiting of foreign brands is a regular occurrence in China—it has been, and continues to be, a problem in other emerging Asian economies such as Korea, Taiwan, Singapore, Hong Kong, Thailand, Malaysia, Vietnam and Indonesia. Despite its magnitude, it is unlikely that the problem in China is on the scale it is in these other markets; at least the problem in China could be no worse. Nevertheless, it seems that the US focuses on China in this regard, and ignores the flagrant counterfeiting that goes on in other countries with which it enjoys a trade surplus. US trade officials, meanwhile, argue that China must close down dozens of State enterprises to remedy the counterfeit problem. This approach simply does not make sense and is in direct contradiction with human rights concerns, as State enterprises in China are established to provide basic living conditions to workers and their families. To randomly close down factories as a way of addressing counterfeit problems would result in massive unemployment and dislocation of labour, which in itself would be a violation of human rights.

China's eventual accession to the World Trade Organization and its emergence as an important exporter on the world's markets is something which cannot be avoided. The machinery, somewhat modelled on Japan's own trade promotion policies, is already in motion. The adoption of a 'containment' policy by the US and some of its European allies may irritate or, at the most, frustrate this momentum for a while. It cannot, however, block China's inevitable and natural path of growth.

Intellectual property protection

While US trade officials are always quick to launch criticisms at China's efforts to develop a legal system, they seem slow to recognise that, within only 10 years, China has put in place a system of intellectual property protection which most Western nations took decades (and in some cases, centuries) to develop. To a great extent, this rapid development was to protect the rights of foreign investors and to encourage investment in China as part of China's open door policy. Foreign expertise and opinions have been sought throughout the entire process; China should be applauded in this regard, not attacked.

Intellectual property rights can be enforced in China by working within the existing system. Many foreign multinationals have succeeded in this regard, although their success stories fail to make international press headlines. Multinationals seeking to protect their intellectual property rights can seek assistance directly with the authorities concerned, namely the State Administration of Industry and Commerce and the National Copyright Administration, at the State level and through regional branches. At the local level, these organisations often do not have the trained manpower to identify counterfeits and would find foreign assistance useful. A proactive approach of working with these authorities, rather than making empty, misguided threats against them, could achieve wonders. To some degree, failures to protect intellectual property rights stem from failures to use the system that is in place.

Foreign investment incentives

Up until 1996, foreign investment incentives involved duty exemptions for capital equipment and materials imported for investment purposes. Duties on imported finished goods, however, have remained high, to the chagrin of foreign multinationals who may not be as interested in investing in production facilities in China as in simply selling finished commodities there.

Chinese President Jiang Zemin startled the international community when he announced at the 1995 Asia Pacific Economic Cooperation Leaders' Conference that, in 1996, China would slash import duties by some 30% on over 4000 of some 6000 items which China imports, and would also eliminate quota, licensing and other import controls on approximately 170 tariff categories, accounting for over 30% of the commodities now subject to import quotas and licensing requirements.

These moves were followed by the cancellation of the exemption for capital imports in connection with foreign investment. When foreign investors complained that China was 'no longer encouraging investment', China made it clear that its intention was to remove the discrepancies in investment incentives between foreign and domestic enterprises, while at the same time dropping trade barriers. Overall, the country was introducing a more balanced commercial atmosphere for both foreign and domestic concerns. Then followed announcements that China would allow foreign companies to establish trading corporations, initially on an experimental basis in the special Waigaoqiao area of Pudong Special Zone in Shanghai. This move in itself is a significant development: while in the past exports have always been encouraged, trading activities as such have remained a sacrosanct realm of State control.

MEMBERSHIP OF WTO

American trade officials have put forward a number of conditions and proposals for China's entry into the WTO. In the early summer of 1994, then US Ambassador Stepleton Roy presented China with a draft 'Accession Protocol' for China to follow as a preliminary to its entry to the WTO. Taking the proposal seriously, a Chinese delegation travelled to Washington in August of that year to discuss it with the United States Trade Representative (USTR), Mickey Kantor, and other US officials, only to be told that the proposal given to the Chinese by Ambassador Roy was that of the previous USTR, and so they would have to start from scratch. This was not appreciated by the Chinese. Owing to its system of government, China has much greater continuity in the personnel handling such negotiations. Most of the China teams have been involved in the WTO negotiations from the time China applied in 1986 (at that time, to the GATT).

John C. Leonard, an American attorney living in Hong Kong who specialises on WTO matters, has commented:

> Contrast the Chinese situation to that of the US change of national government every four years with consequent changes not only of the USTR, but also presumably of many of the support staff involved in these discussions. The result is what we have: a continuing stalemate resulting from changing signals from different personnel of different US administrations (of different political persuasions). The only consistency in US policy on the China/WTO issue is the fact that the US is blocking China from WTO for technical, trade-related publicly disseminated reasons, while at the same time, in my opinion, the hidden agenda is of course to contain China, perhaps as much in a psychological as well as in a power politics fashion. It's back to the nineteenth century!

Philosophical differences partly explain the behaviour of US trade representatives, who mix unrelated issues with heated emotionalism in their trade dealings with China. Certain traditional attitudes which began with British Emissary Lord Macartney live on today.

Ambassador Charlene Barshefsky, who at the time was Deputy US Trade Representative, provided to MOFTEC and other Chinese officials the so-called 'Road Map', pursuant to which the US feels that China could move closer to entry to the WTO (and GATT 1994), during the week of 6 November 1995. The following week, she made a speech in Hong Kong to the Hong Kong General Chamber of Commerce entitled 'Trade in a New Era: Opportunities and Obstacles'. In her speech, she made reference to the Road Map, describing it as '. . . a commercially viable accession package and at the same time . . . realistic'.

As one MOFTEC official commented, 'Yes, it is a Road Map . . . however, we really do not know where it will lead us . . . maybe if we follow the Road Map, each of the 28 steps will take five years. We could, in accordance with America's intentions, then accede to WTO 100 years from now!' Barshefsky is now US Trade Representative; Mickey Kantor is now Secretary of Commerce.

In 1995, US trade officials called upon MOFTEC to shut down factories in southern China which were allegedly manufacturing counterfeit products; they claimed that, in failing to do so, China was not cooperating or 'playing fair'. Under China's program of decentralisation and separation of politics from economics, these factories were, in general terms, responsible for their own actions. Furthermore, issues relating to the closure of State enterprises rest with the State Commission for the Reform of Economic Systems and the State Economy and Trade Commission, not with MOFTEC. The closure of State enterprises raises with it issues of unemployment and cannot be dealt with by a simple brush stroke.

While it has been acknowledged that piracy does exist in China, the situation is no worse than in many other countries of Asia. Maybe there is some correlation between the demands being made by US negotiators and America's widening trade deficit with China: this may in fact be at the root of the ongoing dispute.

The signing of the 1995 accord on intellectual property protection, between the US and China, relieved many investors, traders and entrepreneurs who were worried about the outbreak of a trade war, but their relief was short-lived. Although this particular dispute over intellectual property was settled, US trade officials continued to use intellectual property to maintain pressure on China, threatening in 1996 to adopt 301 sanctions. In May 1996, Washington threatened to hit China with US$2 billion in trade sanctions, claiming China failed to live up to the 1995 intellectual property agreement. Simultaneously, American computer software giant Microsoft praised Chinese officials for closing a counterfeiting operation in Guilin and confiscating more than 5500 CD-ROMs.

Madame Zhang Yuejiao, Director of the Treaty and Law Department of MOFTEC, has repeatedly explained to US trade officials to the point of exasperation how China has been fighting piracy, closing counterfeiting operations, increasing crackdowns and inspections, strengthening border controls and expanding market access. In reflecting on the relentless pressure from the US, despite China's continued and good faith efforts, Zhang queried, 'Under such circumstances, you have to ask: What's the goal? Is it to protect intellectual property rights, or is there another goal?' The cold fact of the matter is that from 1984 through 1994, US annual exports to China rose from US$3 billion to US$8.8 billion. That is pretty good. However, China's exports to the US for the same period increased from US$3.1 billion to almost US$38 billion. This leaves the US with a US$29.2 billion trade deficit with China. This is obviously the real issue at stake.

It is clearly China's intention to enter the world of free trade. China's domestic economic conditions are now ripe for the country to move from the import substitution economic model adopted in the 1980s into a full export promotion model in the 1990s. In acceding to the WTO, China will finally be in a position to leave bilateral trade squabbling behind and become the world's foremost export-oriented economy.

CHAPTER 7

ENTERPRISES

渙

Huàn • Dispersion

順 水 行 舟 之 課 。
天 風 吹 物 之 象 。

The image is to sail a boat with the current.
The symbol is strong wind sweeping things away.
—I CHING

易 經

The negotiation room went silent. One could hear a tea-leaf unfolding slowly as hot water was poured from an aluminium flask into one of the porcelain teacups on the table. The spokesman from the Chinese party leaned over the negotiation table and said to the foreign party: 'How can you cut so many workers if we have a joint venture? Where will we put these people? Don't you know our enterprise provides everything to the community: schools, hospitals, housing...'. 'But', replied the representative of the big multinational on the other side of the table, 'when we introduce our technology to your enterprise, we will need to sack at least 1000 of the 1500 workers which you have, just to make it efficient!'

Today, China's biggest single problem, next to population control and management, is how to solve the intertwined problems of State-owned enterprises. Originally established to feed people and provide jobs, these economic dinosaurs must now commercialise in order to survive in China's new and very competitive market environment. Some Western lawyers and economists insist that only by allowing these enterprises to go bankrupt can the system correct itself. However, to do so would mean putting scores of millions out of work and dismantling the social support systems (such as schools, health care and retirement benefits) which are considered basic human rights in the Chinese system. In social terms, such large-scale unemployment would unquestionably lead to social unrest which would lead the country nowhere except into greater difficulties.

From a purely economic perspective, a sudden serial collapse of State-owned enterprises would lead to chaos. Today, the cross-debts between enterprises which cannot be paid off leave the enterprises in a morass of debt. The State-owned enterprise system is so entangled in debt that widespread bankruptcy would threaten the entire balance of China's enterprise debt structure. At the same time, with almost 50% of the State-owned enterprises operating in the red, enterprises eventually must be made profitable. The situation with some enterprises was so desperate that, in 1994, in the face of unprecedented inflation, they were issuing IOUs in the form of so-called bonds to employees instead of salaries.

Nevertheless, despite its raft of problems, China's enterprise reforms have been dramatic. With careful planning, which began as early as the 1950s (a fact little known to most foreign observers), China has already made enormous headway in economic and enterprise reform, creating the basis for the future of China's own multinational corporations.

FROM 1949 TO 1978

The period between 1949–78 saw the Chinese economy change from a capitalist to socialist system. In macro-economic terms, this period spanned such massive political and economic policy initiatives as the Great Leap Forward of the 1950s and the Cultural Revolution of the 1960s and 1970s. The years between 1949 and 1956 were especially critical: the period 1949–52 is named the 'National Economy Convalescence of Three Years', and the period 1953–56, the 'Three Great Remouldings', which included the socialist transformation of agriculture, handicrafts, and capitalist industry and commerce.

The changes in relation to enterprises between 1949 and 1956 involved ridding China of imperialist and commercial–bureaucratic interests; nationalising large enterprises; and the collectivisation of private interests throughout China. To achieve these changes, the following measures were taken. Those enterprises in China which had been run by 'the foreign imperialists' (who had been ejected) were taken over, and those that had been run by the old bureaucratic capitalists (most of whom had fled to Hong Kong and Taiwan) were confiscated. Privately owned industrial and commercial enterprises (which soon ceased to exist in nature) were nationalised and became State-owned enterprises, and collectivisation began.

Collectivisation, however, later proved to work against the interests of efficient production. It went against the grain for many Chinese, who took an individualistic view on issues of capital accumulation for the benefit of their families and the accumulation of fixed assets. However, at the time (the 1950s), because of the chaotic land-holding situation that had developed from the landlord system, the bulk of China's masses accepted collectivisation without question as it seemed to propose a better system—or, at least an apparent solution—to what had existed during the late Qing dynasty and the Republican period prior to 1949.

Former companies and capitalist-run enterprises were gradually transformed over this period into monolithic entities characterised by a highly centralised management and control system. The end-result was that enterprises became directly managed by the Government—not for the purpose of making profits or even being economically viable, but for the purpose of feeding and housing the workers through a system of subsidies and government support. The saying emerged that 'the enterprises are becoming societies of their own' (*qiye ban shehui*).

Following Liberation in 1949, the Communist Party permitted a few select shareholding companies, such as Jiangnan Cement, Qixin Yanghui and Luanzhou Kuangwu, to continue in existence, recognising the value of such large commercial entities to the developing country. The very existence of these companies, however, ran counter to the Party's policy drives towards socialist collectivisation, and by 1952 they had been dissolved. The precedent set by the existence of these companies is reflected, however, in the likes of today's entities, such as China International Trust and Investment

Corporation—commercial companies can, through their own commercial development, serve socialist interests.

Experimental legislation

An interesting fact, and one which is, to a large extent, unknown to foreign observers, is that this period witnessed the promulgation of certain experimental legislation which was to become the foundation of much of the enterprise reform which has been successfully implemented in the 1990s. China's surprisingly rapid reforms of the 1990s and sudden development of a full-blown Companies Law should be no surprise at all, as these were rooted in some of the early ideas being advanced by Zhou Enlai during the period of his premiership.

The first key piece of corporate legislation of this period was the Interim Regulations of Privately Owned Enterprises (the Regulations) promulgated by the Government Administration Council, known at that time as *Zheng Wu Yuan*, not the State Council (*Guo Wu Yuan*) on 29 December 1950. The regulations defined the three organisational forms of privately owned enterprises (as wholly privately owned entities), partnership enterprises and companies. Under the regulations, companies were further defined and classified into five organisational styles. Companies could be unlimited, limited, limited partnerships, shareholding companies or joint stock partnerships.

The regulations were soon followed by the Measures for the Implementation of Interim Regulations of Privately Owned Enterprises (promulgated by the Financial and Economic Commission of the Government Administration Council on 30 March 1951), and the Interim Regulations of Industrial Enterprises Jointly Run by the State and the Private Party (promulgated by the State Council on 2 September 1954).

In fact, the organisation form of 'enterprises jointly run by the State and the private party' during this period was that of a limited liability company, and its main characteristic was simply that the bigger portion of its equity belonged to the public.

Collectivisation

Following the promulgation of the regulations, China accelerated its drive toward collective State management under a planned economic system. Enterprise reform as understood within the context of 'socialist construction' was characterised by a tendency to unify the structure of the ownership system behind the State (in other words, to speed up the nationalisation of enterprises); a shift in the orientation of enterprise development from a focus on production to an emphasis on internal political struggle; and the direct management and control of enterprises by the Government through planning directives.

To a great extent, the function of enterprises—as a system of economic entities critical to China's development—was abandoned in the pursuit of political platforms. For it was in the political arena that enterprise reform, as understood within the context of what was happening at the time, was used by certain factions in their struggle to unify political interests and centralise the leadership of the Party.

Concurrent with these moves, other steps were being taken under the direction of Premier Zhou Enlai which (though it was not realised at the time) were to lay the groundwork, and to some extent serve as a model, for future decentralisation and the separation of the management of commercial enterprises from Party politics. These culminated in the promulgation of the Provisions of the State Council Concerning Improvement of Industrial Management Systems (promulgated by the State Council on 15 November 1957, and approved by the Standing Committee of the National People's Congress). These provisions were drafted and promulgated at the direction of Premier Zhou Enlai and gave tacit approval for local government authorities to undertake industrial management.

Along with these decentralisation initiatives, the authority of the leaders of commercial enterprises was extended with regard to management within the enterprises themselves. Thus began the policy of separating politics from management, which would assume such significance in the 1990s.

Nevertheless, centralisation for a long time remained the order of the day. The Working Rules of State-operated Industrial Enterprises (Draft) (also known as the Seventy Articles with Regard to Industry), a document issued as a Party directive by the Central Committee in 1961, remained for years the single most important document in circulation with regard to industrial policy. In fact, this served as the national regulations governing both industry and enterprises for a long period thereafter.

The years 1960–62 were known as the Three Years of National Calamity which best explains the result of the Great Leap Forward, the movement or organisation into People's Communes, and the centralised planning which dominated economic thought in China at the time. Many people died of starvation during this period. China went into a new period of political isolation during the years 1966–76, the period of the Cultural Revolution. For 10 years, there was no industrial activity of any significance—there were few commercial operations. Needless to say, enterprise reform was not a topic of conversation.

THE DECENTRALISATION OF POWER

Following Deng Xiaoping's rise to power in 1978 at the Eleventh Party Congress, China embarked on an eight-year period of experimentation and revitalisation of the economy. This period witnessed the decentralisation of power from the Central Government to the regions. At the same time, the central policy-makers delegated the authority to manage enterprises. This placed enterprises under a lower level of administration, and as the State relinquished much of its interest and profits in these enterprises to the enterprises themselves, the decision-making powers of their managers were widened.

This entire process began in early October 1978, in Sichuan Province—at the time, Zhao Ziyang was in power as Provincial Party Secretary. Zhao began to experiment by extending the decision-making powers within six enterprises in his province. At the same time that Zhao was experimenting with enterprise reform in Sichuan Province, Wan Li was at work in Anhui introducing agricultural reforms which reversed the collectivisation trends of the 1950s and 1960s. Together, the reforms of these two individuals, under Deng Xiaoping's patronage, led to the population chanting, 'If you want to eat grain (*liang*) go to Ziyang, if you want to eat rice (*mi*) go to Wan Li'.

Enterprise reform on trial

Following the Third Plenary Session of the Eleventh Central Committee on May 1979, the State Council initiated experimental reforms within eight enterprises including the famous Capital Iron and Steel Company. Shortly after, in July 1979, the State Council introduced the following measures: it expanded the decision-making power of State-owned enterprises; imposed taxes on enterprise fixed capital; increased the rate of depreciation of assets;

improved the methods of using depreciation; and instituted a full line-of-credit system for providing working capital funds to enterprises. Simultaneously, the State Council instructed local government authorities to further experiment with enterprise reform by selecting a few enterprises in their own areas to pilot these measures. By the end of 1979, the number of enterprises trialling enterprise reform increased to 4200; by 1980, the number had jumped to 6000.

The next dramatic move was to introduce the soon-to-be famous Economic Responsibility System (*Chengbaozhi*). In short, the Chengbaozhi system allowed industrial enterprises, after meeting State quotas, to keep the rest of their production, sell it for a profit and keep the profits. By the end of 1981, the number of enterprises involved totalled 42,000. The next step in enterprise reform involved shifting from the concept of profits being turned over to the State to the concept that an enterprise could keep its profits, but has to pay taxes on those profits to the State. This new policy was dubbed 'Profits Transformed to Taxes': thus began the eventual shift away from State Planning and the adoption of taxation as a budgetary tool.

Autonomy in management

The decision-making powers of State-owned enterprises were further expanded under the interim Provisions Regarding Further Expanding the Decision-making Power of State-Operated Industrial Enterprises (promulgated by the State Council on May 1984). These provisions expanded the decision-making power of enterprises in 10 areas. Enterprises could plan their own production and operations; market their products; determine prices for their products; purchase their own materials; manage their own funds and handle their own production systems. Enterprises also had the ability to establish departments, including those for the administration of personnel and labour management, and to distribute salaries and awards. Greater authority was also extended to domestic operations that were jointly managed by two or more domestic enterprises on the basis of a contract, though separately licensed.

These reforms were further accelerated by the Interim Provisions Regarding Several Problems on Enhancing Vitality of State-operated Enterprises of Large or Middle Scale (approved by the State Council on September 1985). These provisions included 14 articles paving the way for enterprises to assume a more autonomous role in respect of management, and were followed by other provisions issued by the State Council in February 1986, which further reinforced the revitalisation of commercial enterprises.

Put together, these measures represented a major swing, and to some extent a watershed, from the old management systems to a new system of management flexibility where the bottom line counted more than politics. At the same time, this period witnessed the emergence of political conglomerates, large enterprises backed by the power elite, with a brief to invest both in China and overseas in order to bring capital back to China. The first of these major conglomerates included the China International Trust and Investment Corporation (CITIC), which was backed by the State Council with the 'Red Capitalist' Rong Yiren, and later Wang Jun, the son of legendary General Wang Zhen, at its helm; Everbright (backed by the State Council with Wang Guangying, son-in-law of former President Liu Shaoqi at its helm); China Resources (backed by the Ministry of Foreign Trade and Economic Cooperation), and Kanghua (with Deng Xiaoping's son, Deng Pufang, at its helm). All of these enterprises soon became dynamic players on the high-flying Hong Kong scene—soon rivalling some of the oldest established colonial hongs.

1987–94 witnessed an acceleration in enterprise reform experimentation which Zhou Enlai began in the 1950s, and which had been picked up again after the Cultural Revolution by Deng and his proteges Zhao Ziyang and Wan Li. These years, however, were marked by the most distinct separation of enterprise management from government interference. This separation provided to some degree the basis for developing a shareholding system. In short, it became clear to senior elder statesmen and policy-makers that the State could own an enterprise without interfering in the management (except where necessary to sack and replace directors), just like shareholders could in any public company in the West. The incorporation of this concept in Chinese policy and later in law was probably the most significant in the creation of true corporate entities in China to replace State-underwritten, State-owned enterprises.

THE STEPS TO INDEPENDENCE FOR ENTERPRISES

The following is an overview of the steps implemented progressively since 1987 to turn State-owned enterprises into viable corporate vehicles. The first step was in the form of the Government Working Report (adopted at the Fifth Meeting of the Committee of the Sixth National People's Congress in March 1987), which pointed out that reform in 1987 should focus on the improvement of enterprise operations and management. The 'economic responsibility contracting-out system' was duly spread throughout the country, and other enterprise reform programs such as the introduction of the 'share-holding system' were tested nation-wide on enterprise after enterprise in quick succession.

Over the next four years, certain reforming legislation and policies were adopted by the Central Government and the Party. The Enterprise Law was adopted at the First Meeting of the Committee of the Seventh National People's Congress on 13 April 1988; this law made clear the objectives of enterprise reform and legalised these reforms in China. Eleven measures on reform were put forward in May 1991 in the Circular of the State Council Concerning Further Enhancement of Vitality of State-operated Enterprises of Large or Middle Scale, which formed the basis, five months later, for further policies. In September 1991, the Working Conference of the Central Committee of the Party put forward 20 measures and policies on how to properly reform and institute a good management system for State-owned enterprises of both large and medium size.

In January 1992, at a Nation-wide Working Conference of Economy System Reform, Premier Li Peng pointed out again that reform in 1992 should focus on State-owned enterprise management, to transform them into independently operating economic entities, responsible for their own profits and losses. Li Peng's speech was followed by a dramatic move on 13 February 1992. The Ministry of Labour, the Ministry of Personnel, the Production Office of the State Council, the State Commission for Reform of Economic Systems, and the General Union of Labour, jointly promulgated a circular on the reform of three systems—those of labour and personnel, salary distribution and social insurance.

THE DEVELOPMENT OF A SECURITIES MARKET

Following Deng Xiaoping's watershed trip to southern China in the spring of 1992, during which he made clear policy statements encouraging acceleration of economic reform, reforms began to emphasise the transformation of government's own function. In July 1992, the State Council promulgated Regulations concerning the Transformation of State-operated Industrial Enterprises' Operating Mechanisms, which further clarified the legal status of State-owned enterprises and the principle of separating politics from enterprise management. Following this move, a series of policy debates went on at the State level; the outcome was a decision to experiment with the development of a proper shares or stock system on a nation-wide scale. China's State-owned enterprises were beginning to look like Western companies.

Before 1978, China had essentially a 'planned commodity economy' (*chanpin jingi*). All commodity items were distributed, usually on the basis of rank; no-one was encouraged to do business or even purchase commodities. *Touji daoba zui* (to engage in the free exchange of commodities or currency activities) was a criminal offence.

As early as 1981, China began to develop administrative systems and regulations in anticipation of a revival of the securities market. The People's Bank of China (the PBOC), the ministerial-level central bank, together with its branches at the regional level, began to develop certain regulations with the State Council; the earliest dealt with bond issuance and exchange. This was the first and safest experimental stage in slowly opening the system. The local government authorities in the different regions began policy experimentation through the local branches of the PBOC.

The practice in China was to first let the regions experiment while the Central Government observed from Beijing. Then, as the regions succeeded, the Central Government widened the scope and experimented nationally. Shenzhen became the main centre for experiments in the 1980s because of its links with Hong Kong, which was partly viewed as one of the models on which experimentation could be based. Shanghai emerged as the site of experimentation in the 1990s in line with its plan to revive its position as the financial centre of China after 1997. The securities markets were revived in Shenzhen unofficially in 1991. Then, when Shanghai opened officially the same year, Shenzhen was allowed to open officially as well.

In the early stages, people were afraid to buy shares. Some cadres decided to buy shares as it was a politically correct way to support China's experiment. When the shares increased in value, people were afraid that they would be condemned for earning money without work and returned the shares out of fear. However, by 1992, all units, whether government or economic, were using mobile telephones and sending staff on around-the-clock reconnaissance missions to the exchanges to buy and sell securities. This encouraged other cities to join in and, for a while, it seemed that every town in China had established a securities market and begun trading equities in one form or another. Finally the State cracked down, limiting China's experiment to Shanghai and Shenzhen; Vice Premier Zhu Rongji had to fly to Hainan to personally close the unauthorised market there.

Regulation of the market

Foreign investors and investment bankers were critical of the lack of regulatory structure to China's fledgling markets, and of the fact that China did not have enough proper companies (as they understood companies) to list on China's Shanghai and Shenzhen stock exchanges. Critical, that is, until two key documents were issued on 15 May 1992. These were the Measures Regarding Shares System Enterprises Experiments, promulgated by the State Commission for Reform of Economic Systems (SCRES), the State Planning Commission, the Ministry of Finance, the People's Bank of China and the Production Office of the State Council, and the Ruling Opinions on Share Holding Companies Ltd., promulgated by SCRES. The basic aim was to transform State-owned enterprises into shareholding companies across the country.

Within only a month, a series of 12 regulations was issued at the State level to bring about the shareholding system revolution, beginning with the Interim Provisions Concerning Macro-management of Shares System Experimental Enterprises, promulgated by the State Planning Commission and SCRES on 15 June 1992. The Interim Provisions Regarding Taxes of Shares System Experimental Enterprises were promulgated by the State Tax Bureau and SCRES on 12 June 1992. These two regulations were soon followed by 10 more, promulgated jointly by SCRES and other authorities to cover, among others, the following areas: accounting systems, administration of labour and salaries, auditing, finance administration, provision and sales of materials, management of State-owned properties, registration by the Administration Bureau for Industry and Commerce, and distribution and transaction of shares. Investment bankers were soon prowling around the administrative government halls of Beijing seeking Chinese companies to list overseas. Like palace eunuchs fighting among themselves for imperial favours, Western lawyers soon followed, hunting B shares to list.

The Company Law

All these moves culminated in the adoption of the Company Law of the People's Republic of China which was adopted at the Fifth Meeting of the Standing Committee of the Eighth National People's Congress and promulgated by the State Chairman, Jiang Zemin, on 29 December 1993.

The Company Law became the legal basis for the acceleration of enterprise reform, and sparked an increase in the number of experimental enterprises. It further led to an increase in the number of enterprises whose shares were transacted on the market, and to the development and improvement of the legal basis for the operation of China's securities markets.

In order to reinforce the principles of the Company Law, regulations concerning the development of the share system have since been promulgated, improved and perfected with such speed that neither Western lawyers nor investment bankers can keep up. These reforms have led to a situation where the State-owned enterprises have, one by one, been transformed into corporations with a shareholding structuring. And, while the State may be the majority shareholder with as much as 70% of the shares, shares are also issued to the workers and other corporate or State-enterprise or administrative entities who, in turn, can trade them freely.

Protection of the investor

One of the unique characteristics of the emerging securities markets was the overriding concern that investors be protected from losing their money. For instance, a buyer could purchase shares and sell them back to the seller for the same price, as the seller had to guarantee that the buyer would not lose money. The basic share par value could always be guaranteed. The objective was to encourage people to accept this new form of investment and to encourage the recognition of the securities market concept.

Another early characteristic was the separation of dividends from profits; this was accomplished by guaranteeing interest on each share on the same principle of a bank deposit, thereby guaranteeing profit to the investor. This, however, had a negative effect, as people purchased shares and held onto them for their interest value instead of engaging in trading, which could be risky; this had a slightly retarding effect on the initial development of share trading. In parallel, there was a limitation on the amount one could receive as a dividend in connection with a share—too much dividend income would reek of capitalism.

At that time, each share was also issued in an individual's name so as to prevent losses resulting from lost or stolen shares. Shares could be transferred but, in line with the practice of the time, such transfers were subject to 'approval'. The issues were primarily for internal purposes, that is, enterprises issuing shares to their own workers and staff—not necessarily to the public. (This developed later into the concept of 'staff or employee shares'.)

In 1993, Li Peng announced the Interim Regulations for the Administration of the Issuance and Exchange of Share Certificates. These were followed by the Interim Measures for Management of Exchange Centres, Enterprise Management Regulations, and the Interim Measures Prohibiting Share Speculation. What these meant was that, whereas previously, whatever you did was OK if it was not prohibited, now all activities had to be carried out within a clear framework. The new legislation put an end to the rodeo atmosphere that prevailed in the securities markets.

With the development of a more regulated system, trading now must be conducted entirely within the law. In the early stages, the Government interfered a lot because of its concern that the experimental securities trading would get out of hand or take the wrong direction.

The impact on the economy

On the back of these developments, many small-scale enterprises and collectively owned enterprises have followed suit, issuing and trading shares of their own. Where they are not able to list, many of them engage in a kind of kerbstone market, which is one of the remaining grey areas in Chinese law.

The cumulative effect of the regulatory measures has been to inject vast amounts of money into the once debt-ridden State enterprise sector. With so much money flowing into the economy, there has been an increase in production on a scale never envisioned by the State planners in the 1950s. There has been a wide-scale transformation in China's society and economic development generally, with a wider distribution of funds, the increased buying power of workers, and a broader basis for the development of the economy. Furthermore, the reforms have established a platform for the expansion and strengthening of China's securities markets.

The current trend is to allow enterprises independence in business without political interference. The original idea of setting up commercial enterprises which were politically backed was based on the belief that using managers with strong political backgrounds would give the enterprises economic influence and further the goals of economic growth. This backfired, however, because management focused on personal aggrandisement at the expense of the enterprise or State.

THE FUTURE OF THE ENTERPRISE SYSTEM

As the economy took off, it created an atmosphere of commercial euphoria unprecedented in modern China—at least since the days of 'old Shanghai'. While enterprise management had once been locked into Party policy, the Party for the first time took a passive role—at least from the period of implementation. In the boom-town atmosphere of 1990s China, enterprise managers soon lost sight of priorities, using State funds to redecorate their offices, buy cars and mobile telephones, and hire several secretaries to escort them on all their many business trips.

The first casualty of the anti-corruption campaign of 1989 was Kanghua, the enterprise run by Deng Xiaoping's own son, Deng Pufang, which collapsed. The second fall-out came with the anti-corruption campaign of 1995 and the shake-up of Shougang (Capital Steel). Both incidents led to a rethinking of the role of political support for management of key enterprises. The trend today is to rely less and less on political background and more on professional ability. There is, however, some way to go before this change in direction is completely achieved.

An enterprise general manager often doesn't see himself as a boss of an enterprise; rather, he sees himself as a political official serving in the capacity of a general manager. The fluidity of a system capable of shifting enterprise managers to become political officials and back has not, in fact, helped the commercial enterprise system. Vice Chairman Rong Yiren's CITIC is an example: in the 1980s, CITIC was seen as backed by the State Council. Now it is being seen more as an enterprise which is growing increasingly independent of political reins, with many independent subsidiaries both in China and abroad which the State Council cannot necessarily control in any way through political means. Over time, there will be less government interference in enterprise matters. It is to be hoped that the Government will focus on wider macro-economic policies and on developing educational systems and implementing these systems for the benefit of enterprise growth.

One of China's solutions has been to bring in foreign investment to solve State enterprise restructuring problems. Due to mismanagement, however, these funds have been used, in many cases, to buy cars and houses, to meet immediate consumer needs and to invest in nightclubs and leisure facilities, rather than invested in people's education and enterprise infrastructure. If properly adhered to, the policy of using capital from foreign investment to resolve restructuring problems should form the base from which to launch a stronger enterprise system. Along with the adoption of international-standard management systems, the policy should also create a multinational culture in the foreign investment enterprises established in China.

The greatest challenge now being faced by the State enterprise sector is how to become efficient. Efficiency requires relief from the burden of welfare support inherent in the State enterprise system; however, this means not supporting people, who in turn will become a mobile labour force and eventually a source of social unrest. The efficiency challenge is heightened by a chronic lack of qualified people. Creating skilled labour to make enterprises efficient requires education. However, under the current structure, without a welfare system in place, supported by enterprises, there would be no economic support base for an educational system. In adopting a modern tax-based system in parallel with the gradual dismantling of State-owned enterprises, China is trying to address this issue.

China's single biggest problem (next to population control) is how to solve the question of enterprise reform. This issue is crucial for the success of China's overall economic reforms and is the keystone to solving many of its other problems. In order to bail out

CHAPTER 8

MONETARY POLICY

升

Shēng • Ascending

高 由 植 木 之 課 。
積 小 成 大 之 象 。

The image is the growing tree in a high mountain.
The symbol is of small things accumulating until they become great.

—I CHING

易 經

After the Communist victory in 1949, the 'red capitalists' of the time remained, as Generalissimo Chiang Kai-shek and his cronies fled to Taiwan. However, with the experimentation in socialism in New China, even the banks of the red capitalists underwent reform, being remoulded to suit the new economic conditions. All of the remaining industrial, commercial, agricultural, deposit and lending activities were soon absorbed into the People's Bank of China (the PBOC). The PBOC took on the role of both a comprehensive national commercial bank and a central monetary authority. Its functions at this time included political administration, the printing and issuing of currency, treasury matters of all kinds, financial administration, and the running of commercial banking activities.

Command economic planning dominated the banking industry. Policy lending and commercial lending merged into a single banking function; the PBOC was all-powerful. The three specialised banks, the Bank of China, the Bank of Agriculture and the Industrial Commercial Bank, were completely controlled by the PBOC. Effectively, these three banks only acted as branches of the PBOC or as doors to outside customers, often simply administering the implementation of policy loans, loans authorised by the State Planning Commission. The State Planning Commission would approve funds for certain sectors or projects which would be taken from the PBOC and issued through the Agricultural Bank or the Industrial Commercial Bank, in the form of low-interest loans with long pay-back periods, while the Bank of China acted primarily as a trade finance bank to deal with international trade and foreign exchange matters. Effectively, all banks were simply acting as deposit accounts of the State Planning Commission. Within the context of this Soviet model, it was soon discovered that it had intrinsic 'contradictions' which were not suitable to the actual economic and developmental needs of China.

REFORM OF THE BANKING SYSTEM

Following the economic reforms introduced at the Eleventh Party Congress in 1978, the banking system became a key issue on the reform agenda. The real moves at reforming the banking system, however, began around 1984 under Chen Muhua's leadership. Chen Muhua, who served as the first female Governor of the People's Bank of China and was a State Councillor, was greatly supported by the wife of Zhou Enlai, Deng Yingchao.

The central bank

The first reform was to split the PBOC from the commercial banks in order to separate central bank functions from commercial bank activities. At that time, the PBOC, as mentioned, had a range of functions such as banking clearance and setting lending rates, deposit rates and foreign exchange rates, and it also managed the State reserves. It also managed all the commercial banks, even to the extent of internal management and business operations. When, in 1984, the PBOC began to hive off its commercial activities to the commercial banks, these banks were still very much acting as branches of the PBOC, and could not undertake the full range of commercial retail banking activities. The PBOC therefore continued these activities until the commercial banks could assume full responsibility. In addition, the PBOC continued to carry on its own policy loan work on behalf of the State, providing loans directly to key industries supported by the State.

The key central bank reforms, which were viewed as the main issue to be tackled at the time, involved stabilising the currency (to fight inflation) and strengthening the administrative and regulatory apparatus for the financial and banking sector. This was achieved by controlling the supply of currency and the volume of loans issued, and creating parameters of upper and lower lending and deposit-taking rates while allowing commercial banks to work within these parameters at commercial terms. These measures were gradually implemented throughout the late 1980s, creating a basis for the separation and transfer of retail commercial banking to the specialised banks under the PBOC, and allowing for a consolidation of central bank functions within the PBOC.

The policy banks

In the early 1990s, the decision was taken to establish three separate policy banks (the Agricultural Development Bank, the Industrial Development Bank and the Eximbank) to undertake the preferential lending related to State development of particular sectors of the Chinese economy which had formerly been a dual policy function of the three specialised banks, the Agricultural Bank, the Industrial Commercial Bank and the Bank of China. Following the formal creation of the three policy banks in 1994, the three specialised banks focused on commercial retail banking services.

The creation of the three main policy banks in parallel with the streamlining of the three specialised banks' commercial functions was intended to concentrate expertise and lead to more efficient operations. The Industrial Development Bank was established primarily for construction purposes related to major State infrastructure projects. The Agricultural Development Bank is focused on lending to the agricultural sector, which is the sector critical to an improvement in and stabilisation of the PRC economy. The Eximbank is a foreign trade bank which is focused on providing preferential terms to stimulate national trade.

Previously, all three of the specialised commercial banks carried out these types of policy lending, creating glaring contradictions in the system. In fact, the former Agricultural Bank provided loans on a commercial basis to the rural areas as a retail bank while at the same time performing the work of a policy bank.

The functions of policy banks are not to work simply in accordance with profit motives, but rather to maintain stable operations without losses in providing a development function. In particular, the policy banks are focused more on large infrastructure projects for national development and on the provision of technical support to assist the economy.

The policy banks are largely funded by the Ministry of Finance, which effectively means that State tax revenues are used to implement policy programs. Bonds are also issued to raise funds for infrastructure projects. These days, the three specialised commercial banks have three critical objectives: to maintain commercial profitability; to keep liquidity in the system; and to participate in interbank lending and interbank support to create faith in the banking industry as a whole and a secure environment for the business community. In addition, a number of shareholding banks have emerged along with investment banks, leasing companies, insurance companies, stock brokerages and financing companies. Foreign bank branches as well as non-banking financial institutions are now being licensed, including the newly opened offices of China's nascent insurance industry.

THE RENMINBI

In an economy of past scarcity, the fact that the Renminbi was not convertible was due to an established trade system which was largely structured to control both commodity and cash flows. From 1980, the Foreign Exchange Certificate (FEC) was issued as a partially convertible currency principally for foreign use. During the 1980s, it became a tool for rationing consumer commodities—particularly imports—and providing a means of stopping the drain on China's foreign exchange reserves. China's need for both raw materials and technology imports, combined with growing domestic consumer demand for foreign products, eventually made the FEC a part of the regulatory mechanism, until its abolition in 1993.

That China has brought its currency to the threshold of convertibility illustrates the success of a series of carefully planned moves involving experimentation and re-evaluation of policy. The emergence of a freely convertible Renminbi will clearly mark China's entry into the community of world economic and trading powers.

The Renminbi's past non-convertibility must be viewed in conjunction with the Government's concern over the control of domestic resources and its fear of the depletion of national foreign exchange reserves, future Renminbi devaluations, and the acquisition of external debt. Consequently, the policy of allowing the Renminbi to become a convertible currency was considered in the light of China's economic reforms, its trade surpluses linked to a successful export promotion policy, and its determination to open up economically to the outside world. To some extent, China may have perceived the problem as being partially resolved by the return of Hong Kong in 1997, an event which in itself would make China the first socialist country in the world to have inherited an internationally traded convertible currency—the Hong Kong dollar.

Exchange rates

On the day that the People's Bank of China was founded, 1 December 1948, the Renminbi was issued as China's legal tender. After 1949, the People's Bank of China began to fix Renminbi exchange rates against foreign currencies in order to promote foreign trade and investment. Nevertheless, price levels continued to vary from region to region: branches of the PBOC were setting their own exchange rates without regard to the fledgling central monetary policy of the time. On 8 July 1950, the head office of the PBOC was authorised to publish national exchange rates; this was China's first real attempt to establish a unified monetary system. The State-owned foreign trade corporations were soon established, and foreign trade began to be conducted through these entities.

In line with the Soviet-style command economics of the time, the exchange rate was then fixed based on a weighted average of three apparently unrelated and irrelevant factors: the costs of major export goods traded in volume, a profit margin for private traders, and an index of daily essentials for a family of four. The result was that exchange rates were adjusted whenever it was felt necessary, and large fluctuations were frequent.

From the 1950s through to the mid-1970s, all foreign trade activities were planned by the State. Foreign trade corporations bought products from factories at domestic prices and adjusted them upwards for export. Earned foreign exchange was deposited with the

Bank of China, and domestic producers were paid in Renminbi. China's policy was to maintain stable Renminbi exchange rates: between 1953 and 1972, the rate was adjusted only twice in response to official devaluations of sterling in 1967 and the US dollar in 1971.

In 1973, when Western countries adopted the floating-rate system which allowed rates to float in response to supply-and-demand fluctuations in the international currency markets, China was left without any system of fixing its own exchange rate in response to official foreign rates. On the one hand, policy-makers realised that, to promote foreign trade, the Renminbi's movements would have to match the fluctuations of international currencies. On the other hand, China's economy remained fairly insular largely due to its isolation in the international community. It was therefore considered desirable to avoid compromising China's insularity if it meant bowing to external pressures.

Legislation on foreign exchange issues

Because China's external relations were rather limited prior to 1979, foreign exchange inflow and outflow was also very limited. Consequently, there was no need for legislation governing foreign exchange, and many other issues.

When the Eleventh National Party Congress decided in 1978 to implement a new policy emphasising economic development and a role for foreign investment in a more open economy, the need for legislation to address foreign exchange issues became immediate and pressing. Consequently, only two years later, in 1980, the first legislation concerning foreign exchange was promulgated by the State Council, the Provisional Regulations for Exchange Control of the People's Republic of China.

The effect of this legislation was to address the fundamental issues concerning foreign exchange control in the country, thereby implementing Central Government policy decisions. These decisions saw the establishment of the State Administration of Exchange Control, under the PBOC, as the general authority in China responsible for handling and implementing all matters relating to foreign exchange control. Also, only financial institutions and banks which have received proper authorisation from the Government were permitted to engage in foreign exchange activities (at the time, only the Bank of China was permitted; however, permission would be eventually granted to a wider range of institutions). A foreign exchange retention system for all enterprises in China was established, under which domestic enterprises were able to retain a certain percent of foreign exchange from their foreign exchange earnings.

Devaluation

Prior to the reform of China's foreign trade system, Renminbi exchange rates were kept artificially high. The value of the national currency was considered by the country's leaders to be a question of national prestige—'face' was probably as important a factor as any other in determining the Government's policy of propping up the Renminbi's exchange rate. The RMB:US$ rate was fixed at 1:1; firstly, because China did not adopt an international gold standard; secondly, because China did not engage in direct currency trading; and thirdly, because national production demanded that the Renminbi be fixed at the same rate as the US dollar, in line with practices of a communist economy.

In an attempt to promote foreign trade—particularly exports— the 'internal settlement rate' was introduced in 1981. This rate, which was below the official exchange rate, was applied only to transactions between the Bank of China and China's foreign trade corporations. At the time of its introduction, the internal settlement rate was RMB2.8:US$1, compared to the official 'external' rate of RMB1.75:US$1.

The introduction of the internal settlement rate indicated that the Chinese Government tacitly recognised that, in real terms, the Renminbi was an overvalued currency (the currency was also devalued in the black market which sprang up throughout the country). Foreigners, meanwhile, criticised the internal rate as being protectionist. Reacting to domestic as well as foreign pressure, the authorities began to devalue the official Renminbi rate until it eventually aligned with the internal settlement rate. In 1985, the internal settlement rate, having become no longer necessary, was abolished.

Also in 1985, as economic expansion and contact with the West fuelled domestic consumer appetites in China, the country's foreign exchange reserves were drained by massive consumer spending. The effect of this consumer binge, in terms of China's foreign exchange reserves and trade deficits, is discussed in Chapter 6. In 1986, the Renminbi was devalued by an unprecedented 15.8% in an attempt to restrain what the authorities considered to be 'unnecessary imports', and, at the same time, to promote exports and foreign investment. The direct result of this first major thrust at monetary interventionist policy was to reduce, in one year, China's visible trade gap from its all-time high of $11.97 billion in 1986 to US$3.75 billion in 1987.

Balancing forex

Because, in the early 1980s, the Renminbi was not convertible, foreign investment enterprises needed to generate enough foreign exchange from their business activities to cover their own foreign exchange expenditures (such as imports) and allow them enough foreign exchange profits to remit abroad. Most foreign investors, however, were more interested in manufacturing in China in order to tap into the potential mega-market of one billion Chinese than to export. Consequently, China's foreign exchange controls were viewed with frustration by foreign investors, and eventually became a disincentive to investment.

In 1986, in a move to address these critical investor concerns, the State Council promulgated the Regulations Concerning the Balance of Foreign Exchange Income and Expenditures by Chinese–Foreign Equity Joint Ventures (the Balancing Regulations), which were later altered so as to apply to all three types of foreign investment enterprise in China (equity joint ventures, cooperative joint ventures, and wholly foreign-owned enterprises).

These Balancing Regulations offered a number of options for foreign investors in balancing their foreign exchange. Foreign investors could sell products locally as an import substitute for foreign exchange (now disallowed by recent reforms); they could use Renminbi to purchase domestic goods for export under a scheme referred to as 'comprehensive compensation'; they could sell products locally to other foreign investment enterprises for foreign exchange (now disallowed by recent reforms); they could pool foreign exchange among several foreign investment enterprises which belonged to a single investor or which were part of a group of related investments; they could reinvest Renminbi profits in other enterprises in China which were able to generate foreign exchange through their own production (such as exports or services); and they could also get 'government support' in solving critical problems.

The Swap Centres and further devaluations

While addressing foreign investor concerns over repatriation issues arising from Renminbi non-convertibility, China gave further recognition to the real value of the Renminbi when it began to experiment with Foreign Exchange Adjustment Centres (Swap Centres). These were centres managed by the State Administration of Exchange Control (SAEC) where foreign investment enterprises were able to trade foreign exchange and Renminbi at rates which floated within established parameters, somewhere between the official rate and the black market rate. For a long time there was no unified rate between the more than 90 Swap Centres.

The Renminbi, as traded at these centres, soon moved rapidly away from the official rate, sliding close to the black market value. The SAEC at this point began to maintain a fund which it used as a tool to stabilise the Renminbi in periodic trading.

In 1988, the official rate was RMB3.7:US$1, while the black market rate was RMB8:US$1. In the span of just three months, the Renminbi's value, when traded at the Swap Centres, slumped; it slid from RMB5–5.7:US$1 in May 1988, to RMB6–7:US$1 in August 1988. In August 1989, the Renminbi was trading at the Swap Centres at an average rate of RMB6.7:US$1.

On 15 December 1989, in its largest devaluation yet, the Renminbi was lowered by 21.2% against all foreign currencies, bringing the official rate down to RMB4.72:US$1. The move was aimed at strengthening China's exports in the wake of the fall-off in China trade following the events in Tiananmen Square six months earlier.

Officially, Renminbi exchange rates are determined with reference to the value of a basket of internationally traded currencies. For years, Chinese authorities claimed that the system for weighing these currencies was based on the importance of each currency in relation to China's external trade conditions. However, the actual details of this formula were never made public.

In international finance, the hardness and softness of a given currency should be a function of its real value, and not its nominal exchange rate. For a long time, however, under China's communist economy system, the Renminbi price–ratio links with other currencies were less a function of market value and more the result of pure manipulation by State planners. The sweeping, across-the-board devaluation of the Renminbi in 1985–86, and again in December 1989, reinforced this view internationally. Since the 1986 devaluation, in the judgement of many, it appeared that the Renminbi was unofficially pegged to the US dollar. Even after the 1989 devaluation, the Renminbi still remained unrealistically overvalued. The black market rate, as an indicator of real trading value as opposed to nominal value, at the time was RMB9.4–9.8:US$1, with rates varying from region to region.

In order to revive investor confidence after the fall in foreign investment in 1989 and to simultaneously raise the levels of its foreign exchange coffers, China embarked on another incentive campaign to encourage investment in foreign exchange-earning industries—mainly export processing and assembly. In order to encourage exports, China further devalued the Renminbi, from its 1989 official level of RMB4.72:US$1 to RMB5.73:US$1, bringing it closer in line with external economic realities. China also adopted a more international standard of monetary regulation, with foreign exchange adjustments being based on market rates within the framework of existing policy parameters.

By 1993, there were over 100 foreign exchange Swap Centres throughout the country, of which 18 became 'open markets' where daily trading took place based on a computerised offer–price system between the membership. These became a very important part of the Chinese economy establishing a market system value for trading foreign exchange and Renminbi between foreign investment enterprises as well as domestic enterprises.

The floating of the Renminbi

On 1 January 1994, the Chinese Government removed the official peg on the Renminbi's rate and floated it, reflecting its market value as determined by a national average of the various Swap Centre rates throughout the country. On 28 March 1994, new regulations were issued which disallowed participation by domestic enterprises at the Swap Centres, and the use of foreign exchange in payment for products for foreign investment enterprises on the local market.

In a move to further consolidate China's foreign exchange system, and to regulate the Renminbi exchange rate, on 18 April, 1994, the China Foreign Exchange Trading System (CFETS), China's first interbank, was established in Shanghai. Based on a membership

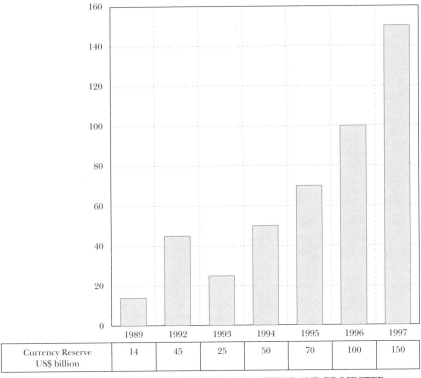

US$ billion

Currency Reserve US$ billion	1989	1992	1993	1994	1995	1996	1997
	14	45	25	50	70	100	150

CHINA'S FOREIGN CURRENCY RESERVES: ACTUAL AND PROJECTED

system, the CFETS administers and supervises the trading at its branches established in some 22 cities at the time of writing. All foreign exchange trading between financial institutions in China may now be carried out through the CFETS. The Swap Centres remain in effect as an interim solution for foreign investment enterprises; local enterprises, however, are still barred from trading at them.

On 1 April 1996, new Regulations on Foreign Exchange Control were issued replacing the old provisional regulations which had been in effect since 1980. These new regulations laid down the legal platform for convertibility. The first real experiment in convertibility began as part of a pilot project for over-the-counter trading at commercial banks. In 1996, banks in the designated cities of Dalian, Shanghai and Shenzhen began over-the-counter trading for foreign investment enterprises. By July 1996, this system of convertibility through 'capital accounts' was expanded to all foreign investment enterprises throughout China.

Streamlining the Foreign Exchange System

Since 1993, then, a range of measures have been introduced to streamline China's foreign exchange system. Their main objectives can be summarised as follows:

- The unification of the variable market rates at which the Renminbi is traded at over 100 foreign exchange adjustment centres (Swap Centres) throughout China.
- The official floating of the Renminbi rate based on a national market average taken from the various Swap Centre rates.
- The phasing-out of the Foreign Exchange Certificate as an interim currency used by foreign visitors and representative offices.
- The creation of the China Foreign Trading System, an interbank swap market in Shanghai, to be followed by the phasing-out of the Swap Centres. Several regional interbank swap markets have recently been created under CFETS.
- The introduction of over-the-counter trading at the commercial banks.
- Preparation for the introduction of a foreign exchange futures market.

Renminbi convertibility is consistent with China's goals of increasing inward foreign investment and expanding international trade. The speed with which China was able to move towards convertibility was, to a large extent, due to its ability to successfully handle a number of critical issues. It has been able to control inflation, retain an overall trade surplus and maintain a consistently high level of foreign exchange reserves. China has also successfully pursued a policy of monetary intervention within the context of a transitional economy seeking to achieve a natural balance between State planning and market orientation.

Through careful monetary management, therefore, China has moved consistently towards making the Renminbi convertible. Further careful management may result in more currency devaluations as confidence grows over the level of foreign exchange reserves. China now has reserves of US$90 billion (at the time of writing). These will be increased to US$150 billion in 1997 with the reabsorption of Hong Kong; currency convertibility is expected to occur at the same time. Currency convertibility will pave the way for China to accede to the World Trade Organization and take its place alongside the world's international trading powers. It will then be in a position to become the world's foremost export-oriented economy.

1. Yanan, 1942. Mao Zedong lecturing cadres.

2. Yanan, 1944. Mao Zedong reviewing Red Army forces.

3. Yanan, 1944. Mao Zedong greeting Hurley Stilwell of the US.

4. Shanghai, 1951. Mao Zedong dining with Rong Yiren.

5. Beijing, 1966. Mao Zedong greeting Red Guards.

6. Beijing, 1996. Young people in a Beijing disco.

7. Beijing, 1975. Zhou Enlai announcing the 'Four Modernisations'.

8. Beijing, 1978. Chen Yun and Deng Xiaoping at the Eleventh Party Congress.

9. 1984. Wan Li chatting with a rural family about reforms.

10. Beijing, 1987. Deng Xiaoping at the Thirteenth Party Congress.

11. Beijing, 1989. Jiang Zemin and Deng Xiaoping.

12. Shenzhen, 1992. Deng Xiaoping on his historic trip south.

13. Beijing, 1993. Zhu Rongji discussing financial reforms.

14. Beijing, 1994. Wu Yi signing a Sino–US trade agreement.

15. 1995. Members of the Central Military Commission.

16. Beijing, 1995. Li Peng with Vice Premiers of the State Council.

17. Beijing, 1996. Zhu Rongji and Jiang Zemin.

18. Beijing, 1996. Members of the powerful Politburo Standing Committee.

PART III

GREATER CHINA

天　下　大　事　。
合　久　必　分　。
分　久　必　合　。

Of all great events under heaven,
when united for long there must be separation,
when separated long there must be re-unification.

—Romance of the Three Kingdoms

CHAPTER 9

HONG KONG AND MACAO

旅

Lǚ • Traveller

如 鳥 焚 巢 之 課 。
焚 極 衰 生 之 象 。

The image is like a bird's nest that was set on fire by somebody.
The symbol is flourishing followed by withering when it reaches an extreme.

—I CHING

易 經

Hong Kong people have never been much interested in politics; they have always been interested in money, however. There can be no question that business has always been the dominating interest in Hong Kong and this is unlikely to change in 1997. The general and unfortunately simplistic impression that the West has gained in the lead-up to 1997 could be epitomised by the following conversation the author had with a US Commerce Department official.

'Will you stay in Hong Kong after 1997?' he asked

'Of course. Why not?' I replied.

'But in 1997 it will be taken over by China. They are communists, you know,' he added.

'So what? Why should it make a difference?'

'Hong Kong is capitalist. If the Chinese communists take it over, it will become communist. What will happen to free commercial activity?'

'Look,' I replied, 'I am sorry to enlighten you to the fact that the single most commercially minded country in the world today is the People's Republic of China. If you don't believe me, then just get on a train in Hong Kong and go across the border to Shenzhen and look around for yourself!'

THE SUDDEN ENTHUSIASM FOR DEMOCRACY

Recently, a lot of hype built up over the future of Hong Kong's Legislative Council, historically a rubber stamp for British policies. These policies in the past were determined by the British-appointed governor's Executive Council, which consisted of bureaucrats and representatives of the dominant business players in the community, also appointed by Britain. In colonial Hong Kong, these posts were traditionally reserved for representatives of Swire and Jardines, the 'princely hongs' which established their dominance over Hong Kong's economy following the Opium Wars. The other dominant player was the Hong Kong and Shanghai Banking Corporation, another British colonial institution which has served dual roles as both the largest commercial bank and the community's central bank. Traditionally, the Hong Kong Club was known by locals as the 'Hong Kong Government'. A classic colonial institution, the Hong Kong Club was the meeting place for the British hongs and their senior colonial government counterparts, and local lore had it that speeches delivered at the Legislative Council were written in the top floor chambers of the Hong Kong and Shanghai Banking Corporation. All this was complacently accepted by everybody—until very recently.

The 'order of the day' changed with the arrival of Governor Chris Patten in 1991. Up until then, China and Britain had been laying the foundations for a smooth 1997 transition, culminating in the Basic Law—a constitutional framework for the future Hong Kong. Patten's arrival marked Britain's attempt to dismantle this framework. He launched a series of campaigns aimed at promoting Western 'democratic institutions' in Hong Kong. He advocated a largely popularly elected Legislative Council with the term of legislative councillors

bridging 1997, and spent much of his time promoting these initiatives in Washington DC and London. He seemed very concerned
with the views of Washington and London, but oblivious to the views
of Beijing.

Was Patten personally seeking to mould his own political future
post-1997 on his pre-1997 activities, or was he acting on strict instruc-
tions from Whitehall? Maybe both. Regardless, Washington praised
him as a crusader for 'democracy' and London used his 'political
reforms' as bargaining chips over the key airport infrastructure project. On the subject of infrastructure, it is not hard to understand
China's objections to such projects as the new airport on Lantau
Island. This is a massive undertaking, yet it is only one example of
the construction that is going on around Hong Kong Harbour that
necessitates filling in the sea. These projects, carried out by overseas
consortia including British firms, have the effect of draining Hong
Kong's foreign exchange reserves on the back of 'Crown land'.
China naturally wishes Hong Kong's reserves to stay—if not intact,
then at least in good shape. Britain's main concern seems to be to
take out as much as possible before leaving. It is little surprise that
Lu Ping, Director of the State Council's Hong Kong and Macao
Affairs Office, publicly accused Britain of wanting to strip Hong
Kong of its foreign exchange by asking, 'Why don't you tell the Hong
Kong people the truth?'

For nearly a century of British administration of Hong Kong,
Britain maintained strict political controls through security legislation allowing the arrest and detention of anyone deemed subversive.
Police had the power to stop anyone in Hong Kong at any time without warning to review the status of that individual's identity card, and
detain them at discretion. Foreign students on exchange programs
at Hong Kong universities in the past were given the following lec-
ture on arrival: 'Hong Kong is a free place in almost every respect.
As an American student you will enjoy it. However, there are two
things you are strictly forbidden from engaging in here: drugs and
any form of political dissension or protest. If you do, we will throw
you out of the colony immediately.'

After having maintained such strict controls over political activity
for so long, why did Britain try to initiate 'democratic reforms' just
five years before handing Hong Kong back to China? In fact, the current democratic reforms introduced by Governor Patten are aimed
at disrupting a program which involved 10 years of work between

China and Britain. This program envisioned the gradual democratic development of the future Hong Kong Special Administrative Region's legislative body. In 1995, it was envisaged that there would be 20 directly elected members, 30 members elected by 'functional constituencies' and 10 by electoral college. ('Functional constituencies' refer to the mercantilist business groupings such as lawyers, accountants and industrialists—a carry-over from the colonial days in Shanghai when groups of businessmen ruled through setting policy and controlling prices.) The original program meant that there would be 40 indirectly elected members from 21 functional constituencies. What Patten sought to do was define nine new constituencies which would have meant that 39 out of the 60 members were directly elected, as opposed to the 20 originally envisaged. China viewed this as a breach of understanding between itself and Britain, and a rolling-back of over a decade of careful work. The original formula developed by China was actually quite reasonable, given that throughout Hong Kong's history—or until recently—no directly elected members were permitted. The only members were those appointed by the British government or the 'constituencies'.

HONG KONG CRUSADES

Governor Patten's initiatives have been endorsed and built on by a group of Western-thinking Hong Kong Chinese, such as Christine Lo, who was personally appointed to the Legislative Council by Patten himself, and Martin Lee, a barrister. Like Patten, Lee has spent an enormous amount of time campaigning for 'human rights' and 'democracy' in Hong Kong—in the United States. Martin Lee has been praised for his outspoken criticism of China, his efforts earning him in 1995 a 'human rights' award from the American Bar Association. Such an award probably came as no surprise to him, since he was preaching to the converted, but what probably did come as a surprise was the reception he got at Columbia University on another trip a year later. In 1996, Lee was invited to speak at this New York institution; he was greeted (according to a report in the *South China Morning Post*) by the Chinese characters for 'British running dog' written by the Chinese students all over the notices that had been put up around the campus advertising his visit.

Martin Lee's efforts, his speeches on 'democracy' and 'human rights', are focused on the West but, since the West is won, his motives and priorities are curious, to say the least. In his crusade, he has promoted the rights of the individual rather than the collective interests of those who choose to stay in Hong Kong after 1997. Headlines in the Western media, such as 'Battle with China' that appeared in *Newsweek* magazine, over articles portraying Patten and Lee as knights in shining armour fighting the dark forces of China may sell newspapers but do nothing for a smooth transfer and meaningful participation in their own local government by the people of Hong Kong after 1997.

THE OTHER COLONIAL OUTPOST

Macao, the Portuguese colony which reverts back to China in 1999, serves as a stark contrast to the political emotionalism which has marked the run-up to Britain's transfer of administration of Hong Kong to China in July 1997. While Britain and China have argued over every issue, from laws to the operation of terminals to the reorganisation of the Legislative Council, Portugal and China have maintained a comfortable relationship concerning the transition. When Lu Ping arrived in Hong Kong in May 1995, he refused to meet Chris Patten. However, a few days later, when visiting Macao, he greeted Governor Vasco as 'old friend'. It would seem that, after both transitions, China will treat the two ex-colonies in the same way.

The frivolous and exciting entertainment world of Macao continues to provide jobs and tax revenues, and there seems to be little fear of any adverse effect on the entertainment and gambling operations, which will continue even after Macao reverts to China in 1999. As Vitor Ng, a member of the local legislative assembly, has noted, 'Half of Macao's economy has something to do with gambling'. He also noted that 'Macao has no democratic party like that of Hong Kong', and therefore lacks the emotionalism that disrupted the transition there. Macao residents seem quite satisfied to know that at least half the members of the Preparatory Committee appointed by Beijing to handle the transition will be locals from Macao. Lu Ping has already guaranteed that 'it would include some people holding Portuguese nationality to ensure a broader approach towards opinions of transition'. He also noted that 'Macao is a good example of how we can achieve stable and smooth transition'.

While people in Hong Kong have been pulling their money out and placing it offshore as the local business community gets nervous, property developers in Macao have poured money into new office and residential blocks. While China and Britain have fought over the cost overruns which Britain is incurring in the construction of a new airport for Hong Kong, which will involve vast infrastructure investment, the Macao International Airport is already up and running, handling 2.6 million passengers a year; by the year 2011, it will be handling 7.3 million passengers. Macao also has its own airline, Air Macao, which is a joint venture between China Civil Aviation Administration and Macao's Airport Control.

THE PREPARATORY COMMITTEE

Governor Patten's moves run counter to the terms of Hong Kong's Basic Law which were painstakingly hammered out between Britain and China. Is there little surprise that China has announced that it would not recognise the continuation of Hong Kong's Legislative Council after 1997? Nevertheless, it has received substantial negative publicity in both Hong Kong and overseas. What has not received much publicity internationally are the moves which China is making to strengthen the Hong Kong of tomorrow.

On 29 December 1995, Beijing established a Preparatory Committee to handle matters for the transfer of Hong Kong from British to Chinese administration. The Preparatory Committee consists of 150 members, 97 of whom are from Hong Kong. These members are selected clearly for their outspoken commitment to Hong Kong's future. Twenty-one of the 43 business leaders appointed to the Preparatory Committee control listed companies valued at more than HK$830 billion; this represents 36% of the Hong Kong stock-market's capitalisation. Could there by any better—or at least more appropriate—political representation for Hong Kong than this group? The *Hong Kong Economic Journal* recently wrote that, 'the pledge of "Hong Kong people ruling Hong Kong" really means "business people ruling Hong Kong"'. In fact, this arrangement neatly ties in with Hong Kong's current ruling structure where tycoons (albeit British in the past) always dominated the governor's Executive Council.

The key point is that China is asking Hong Kong's business

community to participate in the future moulding of China's policies towards Hong Kong, and is trying to develop a political constituency from Hong Kong's own home-bred entrepreneurs. The intention is that this new leadership maintains political stability while continuing economic growth for Hong Kong as part of China.

Hong Kong after 1997

Let's assume that the Legislative Council is disbanded in 1997, and the body of membership in the current Preparatory Committee becomes the governing body of the Hong Kong Special Administrative Region. This could only be good for Hong Kong. In its political style of building upon consensus, China has actually done a substantial amount of work in engineering the foundation of a Hong Kong which would retain its own identity as a commercial hub governed by the overriding interests of *laissez-faire.*

'Red' capital from China accounts for the single largest source of investment in Hong Kong. Substantial investments have been made in the trading, banking, real estate, manufacturing, transport and tourism sectors. At the end of 1995, there were over 1800 China-backed enterprises in Hong Kong, representing a capitalisation of US$50 billion. By mid–1996, Western diplomats and foreign investment bankers placed the figure closer to US$60–100 billion.

China's reabsorption of Hong Kong in 1997 will mean the reabsorption of an enormous and powerful shipping and financial centre. Once a capitalist pocket on the long coastline of an underdeveloped China, Hong Kong will become part of an industrial and shipping megalopolis stretching along the coast of Guangdong Province and up the Pearl River Delta to Guangzhou; the various Special Economic Zones will become satellites around the Hong Kong Special Administrative Region. China's vision of Hong Kong fits neatly into the comprehensive 'Greater China' concept—a China with a market economy functioning within the parameters of guided State direction, and peripheral special administrative regions where local economics drive State policies.

CHAPTER 10

TAIWAN

未 濟

Wèijì • Unfinished

竭 水 求 珠 之 課 。
憂 中 望 喜 之 象 。

The image is emptying the lake to find the pearl.
The symbol is that worry proves a blessing to most people.

—I CHING

易 經

Prior to 1949, the politics of the Kuomintang was a politics of hard money and graft in a Shanghai in decline. Supported by the Green Gang, Shanghai's supreme mafia of the day, who orchestrated bloody massacres of leftist thinkers, Chiang Kai-shek was in firm control.

In 1927, Chiang Kai-shek staged a coup in Shanghai. On 11 April 1927, Wan Shou Hua, Chairman of the General Labour Union of Shanghai, was murdered by Green Gang boss, Du Yue Sheng. From 12 to 15 April, over 300 people were killed, over 1000 Communist Party members arrested, and more than 5000 people went missing. The heads of pro-Communist workers and alleged Communist Party members were displayed to the public by the Kuomintang. Walter Logan, former foreign editor of United Press International, later reminisced that:

Personal dramas aside, it was quickly evident what a wide gap existed between the style and personalities of the KMT [Kuomintang] and the Communists. Generalissimo Chiang Kai Shek, for example, invited US officers and correspondents to his elegant home one night for a soiree. Madame Chiang put on a spectacular display of wealth, wearing more jade jewellery than even Tiffanys could boast. Everywhere you could see, there was jade. When one naive American asked how he could buy some for his wife, Madame sniffed: 'One does not buy jade. One has jade.' The Communists, in contrast, lived in squalor. That was the first time I met Zhou Enlai . . . In Zhou, we recognised a burning commitment that far eclipsed anything we had seen on the Nationalist side. Instinctively, we knew who would win.

When Generalissimo Chiang went to Taiwan in 1949, the Green Gang left with him. Some of the gangsters re-formed as the Bamboo Gang; they became an integral part of Taiwan's politics and remain active today. Lee Teng-hui, current President of Taiwan, in the tradition of his political predecessors (Chiang Kai-shek and his son Chiang Ching-kuo) is today one of the two richest men in Taiwan.

PEACEFUL REUNIFICATION

On 23 July 1954, the *People's Daily* printed an essay entitled 'Definitely Must Liberate Taiwan'. At this point in time, China clearly upheld a policy of 'liberating' Taiwan, the use of force being the principal method of liberation. From 1 January 1979, the Fifth Meeting of the Standing Committee of the Fifth National People's Congress issued statements to the effect that Taiwan historically had always been a part of China, but had been subjected to invasions from other countries (Japan in World War II); however, with the establishment of stable relations between China and the United States and between China and Japan, with both nations recognising a policy of one China—the People's Republic—the unification of the Chinese people did not have to be through the use of force.

On 30 September 1981, Marshal Ye Jianying (one of the surviving '10 Marshals' appointed by Mao Zedong), then acting as chairman of the Central Military Commission, issued a nine-article road map for the 'peaceful liberation' of Taiwan. This road map stated that the Communist Party and the Kuomintang should have a third round of negotiations (there had already been two rounds or periods of cooperation between them during the resistance against Japan); and that the Communist Party and the Kuomintang should have agreements on postal communications, people being able to visit their relatives, commercial relations, airlines, and travel by citizens of both China and Taiwan between the two locations.

On 24 July 1982, Liao Chengzhi, the son of Liao Zhongkai (one of Sun Yat-sen's right-hand officers) wrote a letter to Chiang Ching-kuo (son of Chiang Kai-shek and then president of Taiwan), reiterating the points made by Marshal Ye Jianying and further requesting that efforts be made by both sides toward achieving 'an early peaceful reunification in the interests of both sides'. Eleven months later, when Deng Xiaoping received an American professor, he raised the issue of 'peaceful reunification'. Furthermore, he stated that, following reunification, Taiwan could continue to govern itself under its own system, with its own laws. Deng noted that Taiwan could even maintain its own regional armed forces for local defence, provided that these were in no way to be used against the People's Republic. Deng also suggested that both sides sit down again for the third round or period of cooperation between China's Communist and Kuomintang parties, endorsing and recommending the adoption of the nine-article road map Ye Jianying had issued two years earlier.

On 14 October 1987, the Kuomintang officially permitted residents of Taiwan (with the exception of military officers on active duty and public officials) to travel to the mainland to visit relatives. On the same day as this official statement was made, a spokesperson for the State Council openly invited Taiwan 'compatriots' to return to visit relatives.

Between 27 and 29 April 1993, representatives from both the Communist Party and the Kuomintang met in Singapore to exchange views on the reunification issue. The discussion encompassed issues relating to economic and cultural and other non-sensitive exchanges, and travel between Taiwan and the mainland. Issues covered also included smuggling and the handling of criminal matters between the two locations. Four agreements were entered into during the course of this dialogue, involving recognition of notaries public, postal services and systems for exchange visits between civilian organisation, on both sides of the Taiwan Straits. As a result, the exchange of ideas on reunification is now being carried out through non-government organisations by people on both sides of the Straits.

THREE SIGNIFICANT COMMUNIQUES

Relations between the US and China are based on three communiques the countries entered into over a 10-year period. The first and most famous is the Shanghai Communique, entered into between China and the United States on 27 February 1972. On the issue of Taiwan, both countries set forth their positions clearly.

China reaffirmed its long-held position, stating that the problem of Taiwan was the critical issue preventing the normalisation of relations between China and America and that the Government of the People's Republic of China was the legal government of China and Taiwan was a province of China. China also asserted that to liberate Taiwan was an internal affair for China, that other countries had no right to interfere, and that all American armed forces and military installations should be removed from Taiwan. The Chinese Government resolutely opposed any action aimed at creating 'one China, one Taiwan', 'one China, two governments', 'two Chinas', or 'Taiwan independence'.

The Americans stated that America realised that all Chinese, on both sides of the Taiwan Straits, believed in only one China, with Taiwan as a part of China; that the Taiwan problem was to be solved by the Chinese themselves through their own political methods; and that it would cooperate in the removal of all American armed forces and military installations from Taiwan through a step-by-step process.

Taiwan, in fact, was the single most important issue addressed in the Shanghai Communique, from China's point of view. America's dropping of its former 'two Chinas' policy and recognition of Taiwan as a part of China, coupled with a commitment not to interfere in China's internal affairs, were the most critical factors for the development of relations between the two countries.

The second important document was the Communique for the Establishment of Relations between China and America, entered into between the two nations on 16 December 1978. This document announced the commencement of formal diplomatic relations between the two nations on 1 January 1979. Critical to the establishment of these relations was acceptance of the principles that the return of Taiwan to the mainland and the methods adopted in this regard would be a matter of internal concern for China, and the former defence pact between America and Taiwan would cease to be effective.

Statements contained in the 1978 communique established

certain principles concerning Taiwan. Taiwan could be considered a Special Administrative Region and given a high level of autonomy including maintaining its own local military within the context of the overall government of the People's Republic of China. There should be no change in the current social and economic system in Taiwan as well as in its economic and cultural relations and exchanges with foreign countries; Taiwanese could continue to hold their official posts and leadership positions in the local police force, organisations and local government; and anyone in Taiwan who decided to reside on the mainland would be provided with support and the appropriate assistance in this regard. The document also stated that, in the event of financial difficulties in Taiwan, the Central Government of the PRC would provide appropriate subsidies; that China would welcome and assist significant figures in industrial and trading circles in Taiwan who wished to return to the mainland and invest, and would move to protect their legal rights and profits. China also welcomed political participation by all individuals and organisations in resolving State problems through various avenues.

The third communique was entered into on 17 August 1982, thereby giving it the name 'Communique of 17 August'. This further emphasised that the issue of Taiwan's return to the mainland was an internal one for China. In particular, this communique addressed the sensitive issue of American arms sales to Taiwan; it was agreed that the volume of future sales could not exceed that of previous sales and that sales would have to be reduced and eventually stopped altogether.

Under the Shanghai Communique, the United States recognised the principle of one China, and that being the People's Republic of China. This meant an automatic cessation of diplomatic or State-to-State relations between the United States and the Kuomintang regime on Taiwan. While it was within their rights to, since it ran counter to the one-China principle, the People's Republic refrained from objecting to US–Taiwan trade and business relations; however, the principle of one Chinese government, the People's Republic, had to be adhered to.

The principles laid forth in these three communiques form the legal and political basis of relations between the US and China. Somehow this important point seems to have slipped the minds of certain senators and congressmen in Washington—forgotten, ignored, or simply not fully understood.

AMERICA LOSES THE PLOT

Taiwan's Lee Teng-hui visited America in June of 1995, purportedly to visit his Alma Mater, Cornell University, as a private individual and not as a head of state. The visit was anything but a private trip. While the President and Vice President of the United States did not personally greet Lee Teng-hui, plenty of congressmen and senators did. Not only did they greet him, but they accompanied Lee's political positioning with speeches of their own, vitriolic rhetoric praising Taiwan's so-called 'democracy' and lambasting China. They conveniently overlooked the fist-fights that are a feature of Taiwan's 'democratic' Legislative Yuan and that have little to do with what Americans idealise as democracy.

Since the Kuomintang were driven from China in 1949, they have maintained tight control over Taiwan; in fact, from 1949, Taiwan was under martial law. By comparison, martial law was only imposed on the mainland for a couple of months in the Tiananmen Square area during the turmoil of spring 1989. With the lifting of martial law in Taiwan, there has in fact been a proliferation of political parties, mostly expressing dissent against the Kuomintang. The two so-called independence parties consist mostly of native Taiwanese, the Fukinese-speaking local ethnic group which had inhabited the island prior to Chiang Kai-shek's arrival.

The independence movement in Taiwan could be seen, in the context of local politics, to be as much an anti-Kuomintang rule movement as an independence movement *per se*. The Kuomintang's narrow majority in the Legislative Yuan made it essential for Lee Teng-hui to attract local Taiwanese nationalist or regionalist support to bolster his own chances at the polls. The sole issue in Lee's mind was gathering enough constituency to remain in power. His intention was to get US support behind him to generate favourable publicity for the Taiwan electorate in a crisis situation he fully anticipated and, in fact, precipitated. Betting on the anti-China sentiments of certain right-wing elements in the United States, Lee Teng-hui, in the tradition of Chiang Kai-shek, grasped upon the foreign policy thinking of America's Congress that, as far as China was concerned, seemed, frozen in the 1950s.

Political chicanery

Meanwhile, US–China relations deteriorated to an all-time low. A meeting in New York between President Clinton and Chairman Jiang

Zemin later on in the summer of 1995 was cool to say the least. The American side tactlessly insisted that the meeting be held in a building where an exhibition of photographs of Tiananmen Square on 4 June 1989 was being held. The Chinese side, of course, protested and refused.

This treatment of the president of the world's fastest growing, most rapidly liberating economy and the world's most populated country by the US Government contrasts with the welcome given to Lee Teng-hui. A special Senate reception was given to Madam Chiang Kai-shek in connection with Lee's visit. It seemed to observers in Asia that Washington's priorities had somehow gone awry.

Lee Teng-hui went back to Taiwan to claim success at arousing American support. Building on this perceived support (a beautiful replay of the charade which Chiang Kai-shek played with Truman), Lee began insinuating that Taiwan should become 'independent'. These vague allusions to independence were clearly targeted at the local Taiwanese, whose support he needed for his up-coming election. References to again seeking a seat at the United Nations and the support of the United States (or at least the support of some very outspoken congressmen and senators) made great campaign trail fodder. Lee's behaviour, of course, drew strong comments from China, which in turn drew a broadside from the US Congress. Fall-out from Lee Teng-hui's trip included congressional proposals to arm Taiwan, impose sanctions on China, send an ambassador to Tibet and engage in confrontation with China. House Speaker Newt Gingrich openly supported Taiwan independence; North Carolina Senator Jesse Helms suggested treating Tibet as an independent country.

Military manoeuvres

In parallel with the run-up to elections in Taiwan, China launched a series of military exercises in the Taiwan Straits, from the East China Sea to the South China Sea, from north-east of Taibei to south-west of Kaohsiung, the two major ports of Taiwan. Many Asian countries blamed Lee Teng-hui for irresponsibly creating a regional crisis (at least from the perspective of foreign confidence) in order to simply bolster his own election campaign.

China's manoeuvres were carried out in clearly designated areas and were announced well in advance, with the dates of commencement and completion clearly specified. The waters involved were policed so as to avoid any civilian boats becoming caught up in the exercises. In this regard, they differed little from similar military exercises carried out by the American fleet in waters around Hawaii and by the French in Tahiti.

These manoeuvres were carried out against a backdrop of meetings of both the Chinese Communist Party Politburo and the National People's Congress which convened in March of 1996, prior to the Taiwan elections. Policies discussed at both sessions were explicit and underlined by statements from Premier Li Peng to the effect that China would uphold a policy of 'peaceful reunification' with Taiwan. Li Peng also noted, however, that China would not rule out the use of force should Lee Teng-hui try to declare an independent Taiwan.

What country in the world would not adopt such a stance given similar circumstances? Meanwhile, the United States reacted with classic gunboat diplomacy—by sending two US aircraft carrier task forces to station themselves off the coast of Taiwan. Commenting on this, even Assistant Secretary of State for East Asia and the Pacific, Winston Lord, was moved to say, in an interview with *The Far Eastern Economic Review*, 'You have to read the Chinese statements very carefully. For example, Li Peng's statement, as interpreted by the media, has been very tough. But everything he has said was really very moderate. The Chinese cannot be expected to warmly embrace the movement of American carriers.'

China takes its business elsewhere

Following China's military manoeuvres and America's military response, Chinese Premier Li Peng visited France in mid-April 1996. While America was busy denouncing China's position on Taiwan, France was busy signing contracts worth US$2 billion for aircraft sales to China.

In the past, America's Boeing dominated aircraft sales to China. In November 1993, Chairman Jiang Zemin was hosted by Boeing on a visit to America, when China signed an unprecedented number of contracts with them. Chairman Jiang visited the home of a Boeing worker and hugged his kids in much the same way that President Nixon had done with the children he met in communes in China two decades earlier.

However, following a situation where there had been an American naval presence off the coast of Taiwan, one could hardly expect the

Chinese to continue to support an American industry with new contracts. Li Peng's visit to France sent funds in the other direction, with a purchase worth US$1.5 billion involving 30 European Airbus A-320 short-haul aircraft. This was followed, on 11 April 1996, by the signing of a letter of intent to develop a new 100-seat commercial jet. The parties involved are Aviation Industries of China and a European consortium consisting of France's Aerospatiale, British Aerospace Plc and Italy's Alenia. The European consortium will have a 30% stake in what will be a US$2 billion joint venture aimed at creating a new line of 100–120-seat short-haul aircraft. This deal is expected to create an Asian heavyweight in the currently Western-dominated aviation industry, since it will produce planes designed specifically for the Asian market.

The clear losers here are Boeing and McDonnell Douglas, who had unfinalised orders from China for aircraft similar to those which China purchased instead from Airbus. Both had put in bids for the Air Express 100 project developed by Aviation Industries of China. As France's Foreign Minister, Herve de Charlette, explained in respect of France's renewed commitment to strengthening relations with China, 'We cannot today be indifferent, blind, distant towards a country which has posted economic growth of 10% a year for the past 10 years'.

The approach which Europe has recently taken in its relations with China is pragmatic and business-like. While big US companies could not get even low-level meetings in Beijing through US Embassy contacts following the 'Taiwan crisis', small and medium-sized European companies (not to mention the big players) were tying up one joint venture after another and becoming major players in the China market.

A European Union statement made in the wake of China's military manoeuvres in the Taiwan Straits stated clearly: 'It is a matter of priority for Europe to establish a relationship with China that will reflect the country's actual and potential influence at a world and regional level . . . China is a major actor on the world stage and a major economic and world power'.

THE CHALLENGE FOR JIANG ZEMIN

There is no question that Taiwan will one day, in the not unforeseeable future, be reabsorbed into China. Mao Zedong liberated China.

He cleared it of the Japanese invaders and the corrupt Kuomintang. He gave China unity of purpose; he gave the people a nation. Deng Xiaoping led China out of economic disaster. He opened the country to science, technology and modernisation, and the people saw unprecedented growth, a change and rise in lifestyle never before known or expected. He gave China a new economic model and a road forward.

If Jiang Zemin is to take his place as a significant leader in the history of the nation, he has a tough act to follow. A memorable achievement is needed before he can take a place in history beside his predecessors. If Jiang Zemin is really to become China's Liu Bei of the twentieth and maybe also the twenty-first century, he will need to oversee China's reunification during his term of power.

Hong Kong will return to China in 1997, closing for good a chapter opened during the Opium Wars; Macao will return of its own accord in 1999. These were essentially deals done—at least in principle—before Jiang Zemin took power. Only Taiwan remains; this deal is Jiang's.

On 14 August 1996, Lee Teng-hui suddenly called for restrictions on Taiwanese investment in China. Faced by a barrage of protests from angry Taiwan businessmen and a substantial drop in the local stock-market, he backed down five days later. The fact is that many Taiwan companies, facing high costs and tight labour situations at home, view mainland investments as the best security for future growth. With US$30 billion of Taiwan investments in China, and more on the way, Taiwan cannot but be absorbed into China. Economic absorption will come first; political integration will follow the economic. Force is unnecessary—time will do the trick.

CHAPTER 11

RED CAPITAL

既 濟

Jìjì • Finished

舟 楫 濟 川 之 課 。
陰 陽 配 合 之 象 。

The image is many boats making a river a prosperous one.
The symbol is the Yin matching the Yang.

—I CHING

易 經

Following Liberation in 1949, the Communist Party of China adopted a flexible policy that allowed and encouraged the capitalist tycoons, most of whom were located in Shanghai, to continue their business operations. The policy changed, however, as the State began to encroach upon business operations, gradually absorbing first some shares, then more. Eventually, the businesses were taken over by the State; little compensation was given for private assets acquired in this way.

In the 1940s, Rong Yiren had emerged from a family of textile entrepreneurs as one of the young tycoons of Shanghai. In 1949, when most tycoon families fled to Hong Kong or Taiwan, Rong Yiren remained in Shanghai to operate and supervise the family business. Unlike other capitalists of his time, Rong was publicly sympathetic to the Communist Party and its objective of national reconstruction. As a result of his openly cooperative style, Rong Yiren soon earned the title of the 'Red Capitalist'.

When the State took over his assets, Rong assumed several government posts serving as Vice Mayor of Shanghai, and then as Vice Minister of the Ministry of Textile Industry, the industry on which his family's business empire had been built. However, during the Cultural Revolution, Rong, like so many other leaders, came under criticism and was labelled by the leftists as a 'capitalist roader'; he spent the Cultural Revolution sorting coal for industrial use and sweeping streets.

The Beginning of 'Red' Capitalism

In 1979, following Deng Xiaoping's meteoric rise, Rong Yiren was summoned to help rebuild the nation. On 17 January 1979, following Eleventh Party Congress of October 1978, which confirmed Deng's supremacy and the open door policy, Deng convened a special meeting attended by China's industrial leaders including Hu Juewen, Hu Zian and Rong Yiren. Of greatest significance during this meeting was the mandate Deng personally gave to Rong Yiren:

> You take the lead serving as head of an enterprise which will provide an open window to the outside world. You choose the staff, manage the business and be in charge of all matters. Do not establish a bureaucratic enterprise. In the assignment given to you, you may accept what you think is rational, and may refuse what you think is irrational. You are in charge of managing with your full powers. You're not to blame even if you make mistakes. You should manage the economics with economic methods and sign contracts in a commercial manner. Sign what can bring about profits and foreign exchange, otherwise do not sign. You should put in order the administration, managing with fully authority. As long as what you do is for the betterment of building socialism, then do not hesitate.

The first investment trust company

On 4 October 1979, China International Trust and Investment Corporation (CITIC) was established as China's first 'trust and investment' corporation with Rong Yiren as chairman of the board. It had the status of a ministry and reported directly to the State Council. With a registered capital of RMB 1.2 billion, CITIC had a wide range of business operations, from financing and trust companies to foreign and domestic investment, all forms of economic cooperation, international trade, overseas contracting, foreign exchange banking and international guarantees, travel services and insurance.

To a great extent, CITIC represented a new dimension in developing a 'socialist market economy' with very 'Chinese characteristics'. No other corporate entity was in such a unique position to advance, and it soon adopted three aggressive approaches to raising capital. Capital was raised by issuing bonds on the international markets, borrowing from commercial overseas banks and receiving foreign exchange deposits from overseas institutions.

In 1982, as one of China's first overseas bond issues following the open door policy, CITIC issued bonds to the value of 10 billion Japanese yen to finance Jiangsu Yizheng Chemical Fibre Plant. Ten years later, in an even more aggressive move, CITIC issued US$250 million in bonds. On 28 July 1993, CITIC issued in the public market in New York a US$250 million 10-year bond with a yield 1% higher than 10-year US treasury bonds. The bond was given an 'A' rating. Previously, China had mainly raised medium- and long-term commercial loans in Japan and other Asian markets. This bond issue opened the American capital market to China and almost all the bonds were purchased by American investors. *Euromoney*, an influential financial magazine published in Britain, carried a story on CITIC's bond issue in the United States, referring to the company as 'one of the most frequent issuers of the year'.

The corporation's monetary operations saw steady growth in 1993, with major progress in its overseas financing. Three bond issues were made on the international capital market raising a total of US$440 million. CITIC then issued floating rate notes of US$150 million in Singapore. The bond had a five-year maturity period and its coupon was issued at LIBOR (London Interbank Rate) plus 0.5%, the best terms for an issue by a Chinese monetary institution overseas since 1990.

On 16 August, CITIC signed an agreement in Shenzhen Special Economic Zone to issue a 30 billion Euro-yen 2.5 year bond listed on the Luxembourg Stock Exchange. By the end of 1993, bond issues to a total value of US$2 billion had been made, in 18 different currencies, in Hong Kong, Tokyo, London, Frankfurt, Singapore and New York. The funds raised through all these issues have been used in domestic and overseas investments, achieving remarkable returns.

CITIC's overseas operations continued to expand in many fields through strategic investments which include a cedar pulp mill in Canada, (the biggest Chinese-owned industrial business outside China), the establishment of CITIC Australia Pty Ltd, a 10% holding in the shares of Yaohan International (a Japanese department store in Hong Kong), and Metro Meat of Australia. CITIC Hong Kong's profits and assets increased enormously—the market capitalisation of CITIC Pacific, CITIC's Hong Kong vehicle listed on the Hong Kong Stock Exchange, rose from HK$25 billion to over HK$40 billion during 1993. By 1996, CITIC Pacific had a total capitalisation of HK$60.3 billion and ranked as number 12 among the companies listed on the Hong Kong Stock Exchange.

In 1993, CITIC Industrial Bank recorded a 100% increase in profits over 1992; branches in Suzhou, Weihai, Beijing, Hangzhou, Jinan and Shenyang opened. Meanwhile, in Hong Kong, the Ka Wah Bank Ltd, which was purchased by CITIC when it was on the brink of bankruptcy eight years ago, has registered a steady increase in both profits and assets after being reorganised under CITIC's direction. It now ranks as one of the thousand largest banks in the world.

In 1986, *Fortune Magazine* rated Rong Yiren as one of the top 50 corporate CEOs in the world. Rong Yiren has since retired from his role as chairman of CITIC to assume the position of Vice Chairman of China, and Wang Jun, the son of General Wang Zhen, has taken over as CITIC's CEO.

Everbright Industrial Company

The story of two other famous 'red chip' companies differs from that of CITIC in both the way they developed and the way they are managed. Everbright and China Resources have both distinguished themselves as players in Hong Kong and overseas, but with far less international involvement and consequently less dramatic development. As with CITIC, Everbright's story began with the revival of an old 'red capitalist'. Wang Guangying was the son of a Tianjin capitalist. Following Liberation, China needed business expertise and therefore brought back the old capitalists who could be considered 'red'. Wang was also the younger brother of Wang Guangmei, the wife of China's President Liu Shaoqi. (Liu Shaoqi, however, was one of Mao's rivals, a fact which caused his ultimate political downfall. One of the tragic victims of the Cultural Revolution, Liu Shaoqi died in prison from lack of proper medical treatment.)

During President Liu Shaoqi's period in power, Deng Xiaoping worked closely with him, as both shared similar views on how China's economy should be managed after the disastrous Great Leap Forward. Deng later drew upon many former political alliances, and it was therefore natural for him to call upon the talents of the younger brother of Liu Shaoqi's widow.

Wang Guangying was sent to Hong Kong in the early 1980s to establish Everbright Industrial Company, which was registered in August 1983. Wang became chairman, and Everbright soon became a novel player on the rough-and-tumble Hong Kong business scene, making no secret of its mainland backing.

Wang often received journalists wearing the finest suits and his trademark Rolex watch—an unexpected image for a mainland Chinese businessman with a high-ranking Communist Party background. His style was always ebullient and laced with humour. I remember attending a reception in Beijing to promote investment in Jingsha City, Hubei Province. The first speaker was Jingsha's Party Secretary; the second speaker was the Mayor. Then Wang (the keyspeaker and now retired from Everbright) spoke:

> I remember when I was Chairman of Everbright—we invested in Jingsha. I understand that investment is now making money. Today the Party Secretary and Mayor of Jingsha have said if you invest in Jingsha you will make money. That must mean that they are guaranteeing you will make money. So if you invest in Jingsha and don't make money, then you should go after the Party Secretary and Mayor!

With that, Wang Guangying excused himself from the meeting saying he had to rush off to another meeting at the Great Hall of the People. Raising both hands, he left the room gleefully shouting, 'Everybody make lots of money!'

In 1990, Everbright established a second company, Everbright Group Company, in Beijing. This became the umbrella company for the total group of companies. While the Hong Kong and Beijing companies are viewed as separate entities, both in fact are governed by boards with identical membership.

China Resources

China Resources, while often compared by outside observers as similar to Everbright has in fact a completely different background.

Originally established as a private company in Hong Kong in 1948, China Resources was restructured and brought into the fold of the then Ministry of Foreign Trade (it is now the Ministry of Foreign Trade and Economic Cooperation) as a group company in July 1983. In 1986, it established the central office of China Resources in Beijing, from where it conducts its domestic operations; the Beijing vehicle is called China Resources (Group) Company. China Resources adopts a similar management style to Everbright, with one set of directors acting as the board of directors of both the Hong Kong and the Beijing companies. Although these are two separate companies, in Hong Kong and Beijing, they are to some extent operated as separate departments of one company: one foreign and the other domestic. Today, China Resources holds a virtual monopoly over imports of fresh food from the mainland. For example, it controls 94% of the livestock imported into Hong Kong.

THE STATE CORPORATIONS

Today, there are 26 powerful State-level corporations in China; their names are listed below.

Industrial and Commercial Bank of China
Agricultural Bank of China
Bank of China
Construction Bank of China
Communications Bank
People's Insurance Corp. of China
China Shipping Industry Corp.
China Nuclear Energy Industry Corp.
China North Industries Group
China National Petrochemicals Corp.
China State Monopoly Coal Mine Corp.
China Nonferrous Metal Industry Corp.
China Marine Petroleum Corp.
China Construction Engineering Corp.
China International Trust and Investment Corp.
China Everbright Group Limited
China International Engineering Consult Corp.
China Packing Corp.
China Automobile Industry Corp.
China Tobacco Industry Corp.

China Rural Development Trust and Investment Corp.
State Energy Resource Investment Corp.
State Raw Materials Investment Corp.
State Rural Investment Corp.
State Forestry Investment Corp.
State Machinery, Electric Light Industry and Textile Investment Corp.

These companies and banks, although operating under corporate names, in fact serve a dual function: they set policies for their respective sectors and also operate as businesses. For instance, the State Tobacco Corporation sets policy for that particular industry, and anyone who wishes to establish a tobacco factory must either operate through this corporation or obtain its approval for its industrial policy. Many foreign businessmen cannot understand this apparent dichotomy, though in China it is something that evolved naturally. This is another situation which can be best summarised as 'having special Chinese characteristics' (*zhongguo tese*).

The Bank of China and its 12 sister banks are now the second-largest banking group in Hong Kong, after the Hong Kong and Shanghai Banking Corporation. The Bank of China also started to issue Hong Kong dollar banknotes in May 1994. In addition, China's other three specialised banks—the Industrial and Commercial Bank of China, the Agricultural Bank of China and the People's Bank of Construction of China—have opened their first branch operations in Hong Kong. All in all, there are 18 Chinese banks operating in Hong Kong in terms of beneficiary ownership.

RESTRUCTURING OF INDUSTRY AND ENTERPRISE

Between 1985–86, in the course of China's restructuring of its industries, four ministries—the Machinery Industry Ministry, the Electronics Ministry, the Ship Manufacturing Ministry and the Ordinance Ministry—were combined into a single Machinery Commission. Zou Jiahua, who's now Vice Premier, was Chairman of the Commission. While the policy direction was to simplify government structure, these four ministries combined covered such a huge chunk of the economy that it proved impractical to manage them under a single mega-commission. In 1988, the Commission split, with the Machinery Industry Ministry returning to its former status as a ministry, while the other three became 'group' companies.

In 1989, the Electronics group company was restructured. The factories under its control were hived off to survive on their own in the market as independent enterprises and companies, while the administrative departments were re-formed into a ministry. The Ordinance group which, like the Ship Manufacturing group, remained a group company, became known as China North Industries (Group) Company or NORINCO(G). NORINCO(G) is today the single largest industrial holding in China, consisting of not only the ordinance factories which manufacture weapons for the People's Liberation Army, but also of a wide and diverse range of industrial holdings producing virtually everything including electronics, optical goods, chemicals, automobiles and motorcycles. Given the sensitive nature of NORINCO(G)'s ordinance operations, which are key to national defence, its factories could not be hived off entirely to the commercial sector, unlike those of the Electronics group.

While NORINCO(G) today still performs the Government administrative functions for the manufacture of ordinance, its factories are free to carry on business outside the scope of production required by the State. As the State has less demand for ordinance supplies (given the current environment), many of these factories are undertaking non-military production under a policy of 'military transforming to civil use' (*jun zhuan min yong*) to generate income in times of peace. Today a number of special investment funds have been established to invest in these factories; investors include foreign investment bank Hoare Govett and Hong Kong tycoon Li Ka Shing. Multinationals such as Honda and General Motors have joint ventures with NORINCO(G).

Holding companies

As government bodies in China are not permitted to engage in business directly, it is common for them to establish subsidiary companies for this purpose. For instance, it is current practice in Shanghai for certain departments of the municipal government to establish what are referred to as 'holding companies' that are subsidiary to them. (These holding companies, however, should not be confused with the many entities the departments establish to engage in actual business; the holding companies are in most cases established to serve a quasi-regulatory role.)

At the national level, the China Aviation and Aeronautics

Corporation (CAAC) may be seen as a holding company, as it performs a regulatory role overseeing the theoretically independent and separate airline corporations under it. Previously, the Aeronautics and Aviation Ministry ran all air traffic in China, China's carriers on international routes and international landings. There was only one national airline and this was basically run by the Ministry. A portion of the Ministry was later transformed into CAAC which served as the national regulatory body for the aviation industry and then as a corporation doing business in its own right; air carriers were split into separate airline companies with Air China as the national carrier and each region establishing its own regional airline. Today, CAAC acts as an international corporation engaging in aeronautics-related business with a portfolio of very diversified holdings.

Likewise, local departments of government will establish holding companies to serve as quasi-regulatory bodies to administer the industrial corporations under them. In this respect, they are in the front line to negotiate with foreign corporations interested in investing in subsidiary companies.

Holding companies frequently establish corporations separate from those under their regulatory ambit so that the entities they regulate can themselves invest in them. In fact, virtually every department of the Shanghai municipal government has an 'investment company'. Such entities may from time to time establish satellites offshore for the purpose of carrying out various transactions, for the ultimate benefit of the State or local government body concerned.

Most of the directors and/or shareholders of these offshore subsidiaries are established as registered Hong Kong companies, but are from the PRC and not Hong Kong. Companies are rarely registered using the name of a 'Government' entity—names of individuals are used for shareholder registration purposes. This is not surprising as it is often the case that State entities will use the names of individuals as nominees to represent them when registering companies offshore. Many are using the same registered address in both Hong Kong and Shanghai, which indicates they are from the same 'unit', meaning that they are most likely from the same State organisation or enterprise.

Diversification and expansion

Whether established at the national, provincial or municipal level, many State-owned enterprises have been undergoing a series of transformations; the objective is that they will eventually diversify beyond their core industries and become fully fledged multinationals with interests in a number of industrial fields. Such diversification plans are commonplace in China today: virtually every large industrial enterprise has ambitions of converting its assets into diversified holdings with the view of becoming a conglomerate along the lines of the 'soga-soshas', the old Japanese trading houses that are now the major corporations, such as Sony and Mitsubishi.

The long-term plan for many of these Chinese enterprises is to establish an international conglomerate in the form of a group of companies, or multinational conglomerate. This will be achieved by purchasing other companies and merging, or setting up equity joint and cooperative joint ventures with other companies to expand the asset base. A certain critical mass of assets is required for listing purposes in China as well as overseas.

Foreign investors fit into this picture by being the means through which the enterprise can expand—through foreign investment, the Chinese enterprise will experience growth of its own asset base, which would have been impossible using its own capital. Foreign investors who are in a joint venture with such an enterprise will often play a part in a diversification strategy (though they may be unaware of it). This is probably why foreign investors often receive a request from their Chinese partners for the Chinese partners to transfer their equity in existing joint ventures with the foreign partner to a third party entity which it apparently does not control.

Chinese enterprises set about implementing their diversification strategy in a very systematic and precise manner. They do it by transforming the former State-owned enterprise into a company; transforming the company into a shareholding company; increasing its asset base via joint venture tie-ups; and planning to list its shares overseas via a consolidation of assets.

The first step in this process is that the enterprise will undergo a name-change, from 'factory' to 'corporation'. This is significant in China, and not only from a cosmetic point of view. It mainly involves a change of operating and management mechanisms; it does not, however, involve a restructuring of assets. The purpose of making this change is part of an attempt to reform and modernise through the adoption of a modern system of operating, through conversion to a shareholding enterprise. A percentage of shares will be held by the enterprise's employees, and a percentage of the value of the shares may be distributed as a bonus every half-year. The higher level administrative authority for the company, however, remains the same: the Government administration or industrial bureau concerned. The bulk of the enterprise assets remain State assets. The enterprise will then establish branch companies and subsidiaries. These vary; the assets of some subsidiaries are totally State-owned, and others adopt the shareholding system.

The enterprise next tries to establish branch companies overseas, after first having sales representatives in the countries concerned. In order to seek an overseas listing, it will need to further consolidate its assets so as to create enough of a critical mass to make itself attractive to investors. The reason for wishing to consolidate its assets in foreign joint ventures in a third party entity is to some extent driven by the current preference by overseas underwriters and investors for a PRC entity's assets to be consolidated in one vehicle which is in turn controlled by an offshore vehicle. The investors will then invest in and list the offshore vehicle; it is currently the view that this provides a lower 'China risk', while simultaneously providing a clear 'exit strategy'.

Today, through direct and indirect shareholdings, China is Hong Kong's leading investor. By end-1995, there were 1800 mainland Chinese enterprises registered in Hong Kong, with total assets of US$50 billion.

REGULATION OF THE TRUST AND INVESTMENT SYSTEM

CITIC began the proliferation of Chinese 'trust and investment' companies. In 1979, the same year CITIC was established, the central office of the People's Bank of China (PBOC) established a 'trust and investment department'. In June 1980, the State Council issued a Notice for Forwarding Economic Unity which established as principles that the banks should try to provide every kind of trust, investment and finance service. To top this move off, at the same time the PBOC itself began to carry out its own trust and investment business in Shanghai and Jiaxing, Zhejiang Province, on an experimental basis. By September 1980, local branches of the PBOC were carrying out trust and investment business throughout the entire country (with the exception of Tibet).

By 1981, banks in 21 provinces, and in 241 cities and special zones, had begun to carry out trust work. The principal banks allowed to carry out trust business were the PBOC, the Industrial Bank of China, the Agricultural Bank of China and the Construction Bank of China. Soon, local governments began to establish their own trust and investment companies, either with local financing or through Economic Commission offices. These companies were established in the following forms: shareholding, financing and general commercial. Most of these were Government entities; the scope of business which each vehicle could undertake was still being set by the PBOC. By the end of 1982, there were 620 trust organisations in China, of which the PBOC had itself established 180, the Construction Bank 266, the Agricultural Bank 20, while local authorities set up the remainder.

The first problem with Government entities establishing trust companies was the limitation on their available capital. Over 39% of the vehicles established at national level were short of capital, as were 70% of those established at the local level. For instance, in Guangdong Province's special zones, seven trust vehicles had over 53.9% of their capitalisation in the form of loans from banks. The efficient management of the trust companies was of critical importance, and the State was clearly aware of the need to make major adjustments to the system. During the 1980s, three major adjustments were made, each further refining the trust and investment system.

The first adjustment occurred between 1981–82. The trust companies involved were experiencing foreign capital liquidity problems since they had begun to do more than trust work and engage in banking business of their own. This necessitated some readjustments; companies that were mixing banking with investment trust work were reorientated. At a 1983 working meeting of all national banks, the PBOC stated that 'financial trust business is to engage in entrustment, agency, leasing and consulting . . . Trust work does not include loans to fixed assets'.

The second period of adjustment began in 1984 when the economy overheated. Local trust and investment companies had proliferated, and many were giving capital loans and acting as small regional banks. The PBOC again held a meeting to discuss reform issues. The PBOC stated: 'Trust work is the cavalry of finance, as well as the department store of finance, and must be coordinated with the work of the financial markets'. The PBOC expressed the need to utilise foreign investment and technology in reforming the financial system and in developing services in the coastal areas, in order to expand the scope of capital construction.

On 17 October 1984, the PBOC promulgated the Provisional Regulations on the Administration of the Establishment, Dissolution, Merger of Financial Organizations, establishing the procedures through which the PBOC or its designated body (the local PBOC branch) could approve the establishment, merger and dissolution of these entities. In 1985, the PBOC issued a notice to stop new investment and loans; this measure was to try and cool down the economy and to sort out the scope of activities being engaged in by the trust companies. On 26 April 1986, the PBOC promulgated the Provisional Regulations for the Administration of Trust and Investment Companies. These regulations basically established the scope of business and the operational activities a trust and investment company could undertake, and laid down the reporting requirements and approval procedures.

On 5 February 1987, the PBOC promulgated the Regulations regarding Specific Questions Pertaining to the Application and Approval of Trust and Investment Companies. These regulations set out the minimum capital requirements for the establishment of trust companies and the restrictions on their approval. Limitations were placed on the level of approval required. For instance, provincial trust and investment companies required PBOC State-level approval; city trust and investment companies required PBOC provincial branch approval.

The third period of adjustment began in January 1988. By then, 745 trust companies existed; the problem, however, remained the same—trust companies were giving loans for capital construction projects and loans for fixed assets that were right outside the scope of their business. Short-term loans became long-term loans, leading to an over-extension of capital against base assets which the trust companies did not have. During this adjustment period, there was a moratorium on the formation of new investment trust companies, and, for those already existing, a moratorium on extending Government loans and new loans.

On 11 June 1992, Methods for the Inspection and Determination of the Scope of Authority of Legal Representatives of Non-Banking Financial Institutions established the requirements for the selection of the legal representatives of these institutions, and stated the minimum qualifications and experience. The need for strict review before selection and approval was another requirement. Six months later, the PBOC issued a Notice for the Administration and Restriction of Enterprises and Individuals from Establishing

Financial Activities, requiring all entities to obtain proper approvals in order to engage in financing activities.

On 9 July 1993, the PBOC issued a Notice on the Strict Procedures for Approval of Financial Institutions. This was intended to clean up those financial institutions that were operating in 'grey' areas; those not conforming with the proper procedures were to be disbanded. The Notice was also aimed at preventing local authorities from forming or approving local financial institutions outside of the scope of their authority.

At the time of writing, there are 394 trust and investment companies. A law on trust companies is in the works; this law will separate the work of trust companies and banks, and is expected to be adopted by the end of 1996.

RED CAPITAL IN HONG KONG

CITIC pioneered investment trust vehicles in China—it has been the most successful and influential by far. CITIC Pacific became the listed vehicle of CITIC Hong Kong (Holdings) Ltd in 1990, when CITIC Pacific's market capitalisation was HK$1.1 billion. Four years later, CITIC Pacific increased its capitalisation to HK$40 billion. Today it has the fifteenth largest market capitalisation in Hong Kong.

CITIC Pacific has moved quickly, through a series of aggressive acquisitions, and has invested strategically in Hong Kong's future. Investments include: Hong Kong Telecommunications (12%); Companhia de Telecommunications de Macau (20%); Cathay Pacific Airways (25%); Dragonair (25%); HACTL, an air cargo handling company (10%); Dah Chong Hong, a major Hong Kong trading company (100%); HK Resort Co Ltd, the Discovery Bay property developer (50%); the Manhattan Card Company, which controls Visa credit cards in the area (20%). In addition, a CITIC-led consortium was awarded the franchise to build and operate Hong Kong's Western Harbour Tunnel, the third harbour crossing. CITIC Pacific also has a 50/50 joint venture with Swire Properties and has purchased land worth HK$2.85 billion which will be developed into a commercial complex occupying a gross floor area of 1,200,000 sq. ft.

CITIC Pacific's Chairman, Larry Yung Chi-kin, is a mainlander. However, in managing CITIC Pacific, Yung distinguishes himself from other 'red chip' bosses in Hong Kong. While most mainlanders sent to watch over China's Hong Kong interests surround themselves with other mainland managers (Everbright and China Resources are examples where all the top brass are mainlanders), Larry Yung has drawn his key management staff from Hong Kong itself, demonstrating a canny understanding of how best to penetrate a market— use the people who understand that market best. Yung's right-hand lieutenant, Managing Director Henry Fan—said to be the brains behind CITIC Pacific's aggressive Hong Kong expansion—was already established in Hong Kong's business community, respected for his ability to make fast deals long before joining CITIC Pacific.

For over half a century, the British have dominated Hong Kong's aviation industry through Swire Pacific, the last of Hong Kong's two surviving British colonial 'hongs' (Jardine is the other). Aviation is a key industry when the fact that Hong Kong will revert to China in 1997 is taken into consideration. As part of its strategic investments, CITIC Pacific has moved aggressively on this front, first acquiring a 10% holding in Cathay Pacific and a more aggressive 46.15% holding in Hong Kong's second carrier, Dragonair. A deal was done in the late 1980s between CITIC and Swire where China would not challenge Cathay's international routes out of Hong Kong, but Cathay would stop flying the routes between Hong Kong and China's major cities, sectors which would be given to Dragonair which was held largely by CITIC. Cathay would train Dragonair's staff and manage its operations. In turn, the little British flag emblazoned on the green tail of Cathay's aircraft was discreetly removed.

In a 1996 'red capital' watershed deal, Swire diluted its controlling 52.6% stake in Cathay Pacific Airlines to 43.9%. CITIC Pacific upped its stake from 10% to 25% on the back of a HK$6.3 billion new rights issue. China National Aviation Corporation and China Travel Service each bought a 5% stake. Simultaneously, Swire and Cathay's holdings in Dragonair were diluted from 30% to 20%, with CITIC Pacific holding on to 25% of Dragonair, with the lion's share, 35%, taken by China National Aviation Corporation.

CITIC Pacific's Chairman, Larry Yung, is in fact the son of Rong Yiren, CITIC's founding chairman who is now Vice President of China. Yung is one of the 12 stewards of Hong Kong's elite Jockey Club, a long-standing symbol of British rule. His new and strongly felt presence as a steward represents the new and penetrating influence that 'red chip' companies now have in Hong Kong. The new-found strength of 'red capital' is a sign of things to come.

CONCLUSION

豐

Feng • Prosperity is Successful

日 麗 中 天 之 課 。
昔 暗 回 明 之 象 。

The image is to be as bright as the sun at noon.
The symbol is to step into the brightness of today
and say good-bye to the darkness of the past.

—I CHING

易 經

'There was a time in the 1980s when all of us Chinese would have gone abroad if there was the chance,' reminisced one modern Chinese artist in Beijing. 'Today, I think few would do so without a guarantee of basic economic conditions overseas. Who wants to struggle as a dishboy in a Chinatown restaurant with all of the opportunities here in China today?'

The artist sells his paintings in China for US$500 each. 'You know, I can easily get US$2000 each in Hong Kong; in America, they sell my paintings for US$6500.' He laughs as he touches up the edges of a picture of Mao pasted on the breast of a nude female figure painted on his canvas. 'I can paint what I want.' He then pastes Renminbi notes onto the crotch of the figure—unabashed symbolism—and laughs, 'I couldn't do this a few years ago, but nobody cares now.'

The Western media seem to paint a different view. 'Corruption, crime, loss of traditional values, intellectual property protection, human rights—these subjects form the steady diet of Western journalists, who focus on nothing but the endless 'problems of China'. Despite this, there is a small but growing body of Western journalists in China today who do not share this negativism. There is an eerie parallel between the current situation and the frustration of earlier journalists in World War II who found their positive reporting of the Communists in Yanan simply edited out of the published news.

What developing nations do not have the problems that come with development? What developed nations do not have these or worse problems (racial strife, drug abuse, inner-city violence)? The debate is pointless. The point is that since introducing its economic reforms in 1979, China has made probably greater progress than any other country in reforming its economy and raising the standard of living of most of its people. On a drive though a desolate countryside 15 years ago, one would be greeted by wide-eyed hungry peasants squatting in the dust amidst a village of collapsing huts. The same drive today is along a superhighway, with orderly thriving farming communities, healthy children and schools.

However, that is not to say that poverty does not exist. In fact, some 70 million of China's rural population are living at the poverty level. To put this figure into perspective, that is the equivalent of the entire population of Vietnam. While these numbers are shocking, it should be borne in mind that, 10 years ago in China, 125 million rural poor were living at the poverty level. It is China's goal to eliminate poverty by the year 2000, an awesome task requiring the uplifting from destitution of 12 million people a year. Under the current Five-Year Plan, it has placed enormous emphasis on programs to increase agricultural output. If China can reach its targets for agricultural output, its drive to eliminate poverty will be greatly helped. At the same time, its growing pool of unemployed in the wake of State-enterprise reform (and collapse) will not help.

China cannot meet all the standards of the West in one sweeping stroke; but then, why should it? Fifteen years of progress have demonstrated that more has been achieved on a far vaster scale in China on the strength of its own policy reforms and financial management than has been achieved in many countries developed according to the theories of Western academics. For many of these countries, development funding is tied to accepting outright the conditions that accompany such funding. Any one of China's reforms introduced over the past 15 years, if introduced in an

Eastern European country, would receive praise from the West. Strangely, the West stays silent on China's achievements.

Despite the opinions of foreign 'experts' and media reports, China's economy is finally on track. Generally, there are few in China who would disagree that the economy is now, after so many years of experimentation, moving in the right direction.

China's political system has evolved within the context of China's own development. Despite the insistence of Western critics that it is headed towards a Soviet-style break-up, the system has been delivering to its people an average of 10% growth every year for the past 10 years, and is confidently projecting 10% growth every year for at least the next five: there are very few Western governments capable of delivering this to their people. Ideological debates aside, the Chinese are a very practical people. Results like these are a mandate to rule. Granted, there have been problems of inflation, unemployment, and widening income gaps between various sectors of society, but no Western 'democratic' nation is without them. Recognising these problems as the cost of a free-market economy, China's leaders are systematically addressing each of them in turn. What has been accomplished over the past few years in reining in inflation while maintaining growth is commendable. There are few Western presidents or prime ministers who could so much as conceive of tackling economic and monetary problems of such dimensions, yet Zhu Rongji has successfully brought both under control.

While change in China often appears to be sudden, this is to a great extent due to process. A lot of effort, over time, is directed within the different government departments at analysing questions, applying experimental measures and eventually coming up with a formula which can be tested. If the test works, the formula becomes new policy. This does not mean that all policies are correct or all experiments work. It does mean, however, that sudden changes in policies often reflect tremendous concerted effort and consideration. It is this very point which outside observers frequently fail to realise in their efforts to understand the seemingly sudden, almost abrupt developments in China today.

China's single largest nagging problem is how to restructure State-owned enterprises. This problem can be likened to reorganising a vast web of intertwined issues ranging from housing allocation, retirement benefits, workers' wages, feeding the population, social benefits, health, medical care, education—the very substance of what human rights is all about. Many in the West do not seem to recognise that China's State-owned enterprise reform is at the crux of China's real human rights problem today.

The State enterprise system constructed in the 1950s under China's command economy was intended to create jobs, feed people and provide life-long benefits. Its aim was to support small societies within each enterprise unit—a kind of post-Liberation order in a China ravaged by years of invasion and civil war. One must remember that in the 1950s the State-owned enterprise system provided a great deal of order and basic living conditions, previously unknown to most of China's masses. With the transfer of China's economy away from State planning and towards market forces, State-owned enterprises have literally become dinosaurs in an environment which cannot support inefficiency.

State-owned enterprises must be restructured to become efficient, but this cannot be done without cutting redundant labour, which is in turn released into the growing sea of dispossessed—Chinese without a work unit (*danwei*). The plethora of growing private enterprises and small businesses, while a positive development, cannot be expected to absorb on any kind of economically feasible scale China's masses if the State-enterprise system should suddenly be dismantled (as advocated by some Western armchair economists) or collapse.

China's leadership is in fact grappling with this problem. Changes across the system of government, law, banking and economics are aimed at a gradual transformation of State-owned enterprises, one by one, into efficient corporations, some to be modelled on Japan's 'soga-soshas', the major corporations, with State-held interests and others to have their assets hived off into the private sector. The reorganisation of the tax system in 1994 was intended to encourage a citizen-funded social welfare system that would eventually replace the State-enterprise welfare system. Similarly, other State-enterprise bodies will, in order to survive, have to adapt and reconstruct themselves in parallel with the changing conditions and structures of China's economy. The question is, can China's society patiently wait for the completion of this transformation cycle?

At this point in time, this question cannot be answered. To some extent, the ultimate success of China's economic reform policy will depend on its ability to transform the State-owned enterprise system in parallel with or along the lines of other structural economic reforms (banking, tax, law) which have already been deemed as successful.

The great irony is that while China's State-owned enterprise system is undergoing progressive overhaul, Western multinationals, in terms of bureaucratic decision-making and mismanaged expense accounts, are beginning to function more like State-owned enterprises. This irony is lost on most Western businessmen doing business in China, but is not lost on the Chinese doing business with them.

Misunderstanding between the West and China are today most evident in the polarised relations between the US and China. While intellectual property and its protection is always the main stumbling block cited by US trade negotiators, China views this as a poor cover for US protectionist measures taken in light of an enormous and ever-widening trade deficit with China. To the Chinese, the ever-present threat of US trade sanctions reeks of Opium War tactics, of another era when the West sought access to China's market on its own terms. These tactics cannot succeed in anything more than antagonising China and a further deterioration in relations, and only serve to hurt US businesses endeavouring to enter the China market.

China's competitiveness on the international market is due to its adoption and careful development of a system of guided market economics. In the analysis of some Asian economists, it is Washington's system of revolving-door politics which prevents the structuring and implementation of comprehensive industrial and educational programs to revive America's competitiveness internationally. It is the impression of many Chinese that America's politicians find it politically less costly to blame China, and thereby divert attention away from domestic economic problems, than it is to actually address those problems.

Ming Cui, co-publisher and China editor for *Capital Markets & Investor Relations Review*, has commented:

> It is China's huge trade surplus that could be the biggest long-term problem between China and the US . . . But that doesn't mean American companies are not making money. For instance, Motorola produces goods in China and dominates the market, but is that considered part of the American trade imbalance? Or what about the phenomenal success of McDonald's and Coca-Cola in the Chinese market? None of these sales are counted as American exports, but clearly the profits are flowing to American shareholders—and the global competitiveness of these companies is growing. To understand the mutual benefits from our economic engagement, we can't afford to concentrate only on trade numbers.

Today there is no other industrialised or industrialising country so poised to grow and expand on a scale like China's. Given its industrial and export growth, China's competitiveness as an international trading partner is forbidding. Given current and projected levels of consumer saving and a population of one quarter of the world's people, China's market is seductive to say the least. For multinationals everywhere, not to participate in China's economy is not to participate in the world's economy. The equation is clear. Singapore's Senior Minister Lee Kuan Yew's prognosis for China's future reflects this equation:

> I do not see a dramatic change in any policies. Certainly not on one crucial policy that matters to all of us, that is, China's emphasis on becoming a modern industrial nation, overriding everything else. They are not interested in ideology, they are not really too vexed about socialism with Chinese characteristics. These are useful words for continuity, but deep down they have one driving force, the one thing that gives them their legitimacy: 'We the leaders of China are going to bring you into this modern industrial age'.
>
>   Without civil war, without a breakdown, hunger, famine, they are going to have many little Taipeis along the coast, and up the rivers, many little Kaohsiungs, and a huge, burgeoning educated class—engineers, computer scientists . . . they will produce them in large numbers.

If one accepts this prognosis, then why all the fuss from the West about ideology? Why should Western governments criticise China's political system and economic theory when China, after all these years of experimentation, seems to have found its own course? What is wrong with China finding its own path and setting its own pace?

There seems to be a fear in the West that China's growth will somehow transcend China's borders. Old fears dating from the McCarthy era and the domino theory of John Foster Dulles have become a kind of collective unconscious in America. Analysis of events in China seems to take place in a time warp which American policymakers seem to be unable to break out of. A plethora of problems lies ahead of China which will need to be systematically addressed by its leadership; its leadership has its hands more than full with domestic concerns to even contemplate the kind of aggressive threat that might substantiate the West's fears of a past era.

As for ideology—to any meaningful extent, this is not an issue to most Chinese today. Most share certain values which are in fact similar to most of middle-class America and Europe—better lives for themselves, and even better lives for their children. These are the core concerns of China's masses; consequently, Western criticism of China's political system and leadership is misdirected and is in fact irrelevant to most Chinese.

The point is that most people in China do not care about politics for the sake of politics; they care about economic results. This point makes the China of the 1990s different from China following Liberation, during the Great Leap Forward, or during the Cultural Revolution. That is not to say that these events were not important in bringing China to where it is today, as they are within the collective experience of China's leadership. In fact, for China's leadership, and for the current generation of entrepreneurs, these events put the progress so far achieved into perspective.

The West worries over what will happen after Deng Xiaoping passes from the scene; most Chinese do not worry or even think about this. In their minds, the new leadership is already on-stage and Deng, for all intents and purposes, is not there. While China's current leadership line-up may be old and tainted by the events of the past, it is those same events that give the leadership a clear vision of the future.

The question for China then is not what will happen to today's leadership, it is can the future generation growing up in a soon-to-be-affluent China have the same vision as today's leadership? Without experiencing a cultural revolution, or more simply the trials and pain of rebuilding an economy and managing tumultuous growth, will China's leaders of tomorrow have the instinctive ability to lead the economy to new heights?

Already much of the blasé arrogance which has long affected affluent youth in Europe, America and, more recently, Japan, has begun to seep into the latest generation of university graduates in China. They have witnessed the seemingly impossible that is China's growth of the past five years, and now take this growth for granted. The result is that the current generation of university graduates now expect everything at once. They sneer at the value called patience which was critical to some of the hard decisions made 10–15 years ago which have brought about the results we see today. They have not seen—and do not care—about the pain the current leadership suffered to make impossibility a reality. They have not worked for these results, and do not feel they have to. What will the next generation do with this reality? Will they know how to make the future work for China? In China today, many are sceptical and worry about this single question.

ORGANISATION CHART OF THE POWER STRUCTURE OF THE PEOPLE'S REPUBLIC OF CHINA
(as at September 1996)

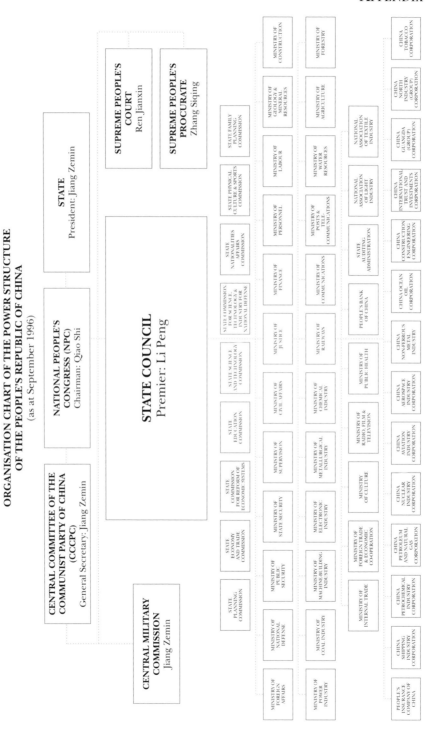

INDEX